YO-BZJ-816

Whiteness Visible

Whiteness Visible

THE
MEANING OF WHITENESS
IN
AMERICAN LITERATURE
AND CULTURE

Valerie Babb

New York University Press

NEW YORK AND LONDON

NEW YORK UNIVERSITY PRESS
New York and London

© 1998 by New York University
All rights reserved

Library of Congress Cataloging-in-Publication Data
Babb, Valerie Melissa.
Whiteness visible : the meaning of whiteness in American
literature and culture / Valerie Babb.
p.   cm.
Includes bibliographical references and index.
ISBN 0-8147-1302-5 (cloth : acid-free paper)
ISBN 0-8147-1312-2 (pbk. : acid-free paper)
1. American literature—History and criticism.   2. Whites in
literature.   3. United States—Civilization.   4. Whites—United
States.   5. White.   I. Title.
PS173.W46 B33 1998
810.9'35203034—ddc21   98-9055
                                   CIP

New York University Press books are printed on acid-free paper,
and their binding materials are chosen for strength and durability.

Manufactured in the United States of America

10 9 8 7 6 5 4 3 2

To Jaren Michael DuBois and his crew,
Sebas and Vie

Contents

Acknowledgments

Grateful acknowledgment is given the Huntington Library and the American Antiquarian Society for permission to publish photographic reproductions. I also thank the research archivists at the National Museum of American History and the Library of Congress Geography and Map Division Reading Room and Rare Book Reading Room for their assistance in locating materials.

I thank my colleagues in the English department at Georgetown University who, with characteristic unselfishness, took time from teaching loads, advising, and their own work to read portions of this manuscript and offer suggestions. I also thank my students, who were my first "ears" when this project began.

Lastly, I thank my mother, my uncle, and my son, without whose patience and help this single mom could never have brought this book to light.

List of Illustrations

Introduction

During the 1970s, in New York City, where I grew up, it was a common belief among some that if the *Daily News* reported that a man had mugged another man, it could be assumed both perpetrator and victim were white because neither's race was mentioned. During the 1980s, many cultural critics pointed out that the term *women*, as used in phrases such as "women and minorities," meant white women, exclusively. When in the 1990s, I offered a course titled "White Male Writers," it was met with a flurry of publicity. Because it named implicit whiteness, it was presumed to bash white males and was cited as further evidence of the radical left taking over the academy and closing the American mind. These unrelated instances, among others, combine to form the impetus to this work.

This book explores how selected American texts illuminate the ways in which one particular racial category so often exists unnamed within a cultural discourse that seems obsessed with race. It does not intend the insulting conclusions "White people are like . . ." or "White people do . . ."; rather, it seeks to investigate how an ideology privileging a particular appearance was disseminated throughout American literature and culture. It conducts its inquiry not by examining theories of race but rather by examining the influence of literature, art, and popular culture in reflecting and shaping conceptions of American whiteness. This work employs a variety of approaches, among them cultural theory, material culture, and close textual analysis, to analyze representations of whiteness in American literature from the time of English arrival to the early twentieth century. It also investigates the ways in which being white became synonymous with being American and what the impact of that synonymity was and is on a multiracial nation. It is my hope that this book will add to existing studies of whiteness that discuss its construction in areas such as sociology, history, and law, by contemplating how its representations were constructed, deconstructed, and reconstructed in the American literary imagination.

This study begins by presuming that whiteness, like all racial identities in the United States, formed over a period of time to meet particular social, political, and economic ends. Chapter 1 reviews theories of racial formation that shed light on the development of whiteness. The chapter cannot be exhaustive and does not attempt to be; what it does attempt is to offer a historical synthesis of existing theories on the making of whiteness in the United States, as well as to suggest particular times, areas, and creations that might lend insight into comprehending whiteness and its social power in American culture. It suggests that whiteness can be better comprehended if thought of not solely as a biological category of pigmentation or hair texture, but rather as a means through which certain individuals are granted greater degrees of social acceptance and access than are other individuals. Chapter 1 chronicles the construction of white identity as the United States evolved from settlements to colonies to nation, and it notes how this identity metamorphosed to meet many ends: the forging of a common nationality uniting seventeenth- and eighteenth-century white European migrants of diverse religious, class, and language backgrounds; the mitigation of class warfare between white laborers and members of the ruling elite as the United States became an economic power in the nineteenth century; the defense of removals and a system of human enslavement at odds with American ideals; and the rationalization of "manifest destiny" and westward expansion as the United States sought to become a world power.

Following the historical and theoretical synthesis of Chapter 1, Chapters 2 and 3 treat the depiction of white identity in American literature. Chapter 2 considers the contributions early American documents made to constructing the explicit definition of who was white and who was not. The printed record of seventeenth-century America reveals language and imagery that evoke whiteness to distinguish Protestant English settlers from all whom they deemed not like them, thereby facilitating two major ends: the justification of incursions into Native American land and the increasing enslavement of African peoples. The chapter then goes on to explore documents of the eighteenth century in which repeated racial, gender, and ethnic representations begin to define the ideal of white identity as male, English, Protestant, and privileged.

Following the discussion of constructions of whiteness in early American literature, Chapter 3 analyzes an instance in which literature deconstructs white identity. Between the eighteenth and nineteenth centuries, the privileging of whiteness in a multiracial nation raised many contradictions. Positing one racial identity as superior and entitled to democratic rights that it would then be empowered to deny to others seemed, to some, at odds with a republican discourse that asserted all to be created equal. The justification of this entitlement on the grounds of genetic and cultural superiority created an ideology that some found discordant with principles of pluralism. Herman Melville is an example of a nineteenth-century writer who dared to question the value systems that made whiteness more than a label of racial classification and allowed it to become an ideology in which the traditions of a few became the standard by which all traditions should be measured. Chapter 3 argues that among the many substantive riches of *Moby Dick* is a radical interrogation of an ideology that enlists art, science, and literature to prove, however speciously, the superiority of white, western European culture, history, and ideals of physical beauty.

Because it is a created identity, whiteness is sustained through hegemony, a complex network of cultural creations including, among other things, literature, museums, popular music, and movies. The power of these hegemonic agents to give coherence to conceptions of what it meant to be white, without specifically naming it, is particularly evident in turn-of-the-century American literature written by immigrants who, though white by appearance, were still marginalized by class, language, religion, and ethnicity. Chapter 4 uses the genre of early twentieth-century immigrant autobiography as a guide to exploring some of the cultural agents—world's fairs, settlement houses, public schooling, and etiquette books—that codified representations of an ideal white identity. Further, it shows how these contributed to making white racial identity the "authentic" American identity.

To study whiteness and its history in the United States is to study an intentional "whitewashing" of American character that even today makes achieving racial parity difficult. To equate white identity with American identity is to imply that whites have a proprietary right to national resources and the allocation of these resources. While the legal privileging of whiteness has been overturned through statutes banning segregation, advocating fair housing practices, and urging equal employment opportunity, more difficult to overturn are the values and attitudes that accomplish in principle what the law disallows, values and attitudes that persist as legacies of a constructed whiteness. Ironically, the notion of whiteness is actually un-American, for it denies the difference and diversity that have always been a part of American national character. Only by coming to a full awareness of the ways in which an artificially crafted identity was constructed to maintain hierarchy and divisiveness can any meaningful and useful dialogue on race begin.

Toward a Philosophy
of Whiteness

Race is everything . . . literature, science, art, in a word
civilization, depend on it.
—*Robert Knox*

It is easy to understand the drama of *Othello*; it is less
easy to comprehend the cryptogram of a
great white whale.
—*Winthrop Jordan*

Whiteness, alone, is mute, meaningless, unfathomable,
pointless, frozen, veiled, curtained, dreaded, senseless,
implacable. Or so our writers seem to say.
—*Toni Morrison*

IN HER FIRST NOVEL, *The Bluest Eye* (1970), Toni Morrison's
central narrator, eleven-year-old Claudia, receives a "blue-
eyed, yellow-haired, pink-skinned doll" for Christmas. As she
ponders the doll, her one desire is to dismember it, not out of
a destructive impulse but rather out of curiosity, "to discover
the dearness, to find the beauty, the desirability . . . to see what
it was that all the world said was loveable" (20). As the novel

later makes clear, as much as attempting to decipher the preciousness of a doll, Claudia is attempting to decipher the preciousness of girls with attributes similar to the doll's. The language Morrison uses to depict Claudia's endeavor is noteworthy, for it invites the reader to intuit a racial category from physical traits described superficially as yellow hair, pink skin, and blue eyes. This indirect description effects a separation of physical characteristics from the race they are most often associated with and encourages an examination of why one set of traits is labeled and valued differently than another. Yellow hair, pink skin, and blue eyes in and of themselves have no special significance, no particular power, until "Adults, older girls, shops, magazines, newspapers, window signs—all the world" (20) give them such by aggregately terming them "white" and privileging that now racialized classification. *The Bluest Eye* represents an instance in American literature where a writer probes the meaning of an often uninvestigated racial construct, whiteness; but it is one of few such instances. In a nation whose cultural discourse is increasingly influenced by race, only recently have discussions addressed the content of whiteness, a category whose centrality to conversations of race is undeniable.[1]

It seems ironic how visible and yet invisible whiteness is in the culture of the United States. Terms such as *non-white* and *people of color*, which lump many racial and ethnic identities together while implicitly contrasting them to a racial norm, indicate the cardinal nature of whiteness; yet, often discussions of race do not examine the assumptions, practices, and attitudes that form its content. Scholarship on American literature and culture boasts more investigations noting racial influences on writers who are not white, and the ways in which these writers' concerns with race manifest themselves in various strategies of form and patterns of meaning, than it does examinations of how literature by non–people of color, or non-nonwhites, if I may, reflects the evolution of European nationals and ethnics into white Americans, and how this evolution laid the foundation for consequent constructions of whiteness.[2]

At this point, a distinction should be made between white skin—the common pigmentation we associate with those we call white—and whiteness. As this chapter argues, whiteness is more than an appearance; it is a system of privileges accorded to those with white skin. What follows is a review of the history, values, and shared consciousness creating this system and of the ways in which these laid the foundation for representations of whiteness in American literature.

.

Perhaps some background on how race is conceptualized in this argument would be useful at this point. I presume, to quote scholar Kwame Anthony Appiah, that "the concept of race that has done so much damage in our era is . . . a biological fiction" that "pretends to be an objective term of classification" ("The Conservation of 'Race'," 38).[3] Appiah's assessment reminds us that though race is popularly figured as a biological fact, it is very much a socially constructed fiction. Its existence depends as much upon ideas, attitudes, and cultural practices as it does upon biological factors that cause differentiation in skin color, eye color, or hair texture. This social dimension of race is illuminated by terms such as *quadroon*, *octoroon*, or *mestizo* which attempt to make distinct from whites those individuals with identical physical appearances but fractions of speciously documentable nonwhite blood.[4] These terms illustrate that, as a means of human classification, race can ignore shared physical resemblance and categorize on the basis of assigned social legacy. Biological attributes—hair texture, eye color—gain significance from a intricate interweaving of history, ideology, and cultural practice. Like other racial categories, whiteness is more than a classification of physical appearance; it is largely an invented construct blending history, culture, assumptions, and attitudes. From a descent of various European nationals there emerges in the United States the consensus of a single white race that, in principle, elides religious, socioeconomic, and gender differences among individual whites to create a hegemonically privileged race category.

In a culture that has traditionally defined whiteness as a racial norm, explorations specifically naming it as a privileged racial identity have emerged relatively recently. One example is sociologist Ruth Frankenberg's *White Women, Race Matters* (1993), in which Frankenberg characterizes whiteness in the following manner:

> [W]hiteness is a location of structural advantage, of race privilege. . . . [I]t is a "standpoint," a place from which white people look at ourselves, at others, and at society. . . . "[W]hiteness"

refers to a set of cultural practices that are usually unmarked and unnamed. (1)

Frankenberg's observations that whiteness is a "location," a "standpoint," and a "set of practices" attempt to evoke a self-conscious awareness of being white as being white, and not as just being an American or being a person. Her observation that the practices that give whiteness privilege are often "unmarked and unnamed" indicates the ways in which acts such as including only the experiences of whites in American history books, and championing these as the march of progress and civilization, or creating literature, movies, and television shows in which there are only white characters foster cultural perceptions that only whites have played a significant role in the history of the United States and that only white experiences constitute an appropriate source for artistic expression. Sharing Frankenberg's imperative to deconstruct whiteness are scholars Theodore Allen, David Roediger, Alexander Saxton, and Ian F. Haney-Lopez.

The premise of Allen's work *The Invention of the White Race* (1994) is that whiteness is a complete social creation. According to Allen,

> [W]hen an emigrant population from "multiracial" Europe goes to North America or South Africa and there, by constitutional fiat, incorporates itself as the "white race," that is no part of genetic evolution. It is rather a political act: the invention of "the white race." (22)

In developing his thesis, Allen uses the example of the English artificially defining the Irish, a people sharing the same phenotype, as a distinct race, through repeated acts of legal and social subjugation. In the passage that follows, he cites many parallels between Irish oppression and that of African Americans and Native Americans, which suggest that skin color need not be the sole determining factor in "racial" subordination:

If from the beginning of the 18th century in Anglo-America the term "negro" meant slave, except when explicitly modified by the word "free," so under English law the term "hibernicus," Latin for "Irishman," was the legal term for "unfree." If African-Americans were obliged to guard closely any document they might have attesting their freedom, so in Ireland, at the beginning of the fourteenth century, letters patent, attesting to a person's Englishness, were cherished by those who might fall under suspicion of trying to "pass." If under Anglo-American slavery "the rape of a female slave was not a crime, but a mere trespass on the master's property," so in 1278 two Anglo-Normans brought into court and charged with raping Margaret O'Rorke were found not guilty because "the said Margaret is an Irishwoman." If a law enacted in Virginia in 1723 provided that "manslaughter of a slave is not punishable," so under Anglo-Norman law it sufficed for acquittal to show that the victim in a killing was Irish. . . . If in 1844 the United States Supreme Court, citing much precedent authority, including the Dred Scott Decision, declared that Indians were legally like immigrants, and therefore not citizens except by process of individual naturalization, so for more than four centuries, until 1613, the Irish were regarded by English law as foreigners in their own land. (46–47)

The many commonalities to be found between the Irish, African Americans, and Native Americans, in this passage and elsewhere in Allen's book, are evidence that the privilege accorded to whiteness relates directly to political, economic, and social factors. As such, *whiteness* is not a term describing an immutable biological content, but rather a term reflecting mutable relationships of social power.

Like Allen, Roediger, Saxton, and Haney-López examine the social imperatives that gave rise to a white race in the United States. Roediger and Saxton particularly cite class dynamics as key catalysts. In *The Wages of Whiteness* (1991), Roediger observes that, "[T]he pleasures of whiteness could function as a 'wage' for white workers. That is, status and privileges conferred by race could be used to make up for alienating and exploitative class relationships"(13). In addition to investigating the psychic compensation whiteness afforded white laborers in an emerging capitalist economy, Roediger examines popular cultural products such as minstrelsy and traveling theater and their role in crystallizing conceptions of what constituted whiteness vis-à-vis what constituted blackness.

Like Roediger, Saxton, in *The Rise and Fall of the White Republic* (1990), offers a class-based analysis of whiteness as he traces how the tensions between Whig republicanism and Jacksonian democracy influenced manipulations of whiteness through the political upheavals of the Civil War, Reconstruction, and the Jacksonian era, where "Whiteness . . . came to symbolize the solidarity of producers against those who prospered at the producers' expense by conniving with and manipulating racially subordinated populations" (298).[5] Saxton extends his exploration by considering how popular white figures—the Yankee and the frontiersman among them—gained cultural prominence through mass-marketed products such as paperbooks, newspapers, and tent theater, and how their appeal shaped conceptions of whiteness.

Ian F. Haney-López extends these examinations to the field of law by noting how various cases attempted to establish legal definitions of what constituted whiteness. In *White by Law* (1996), he explores the "central role law plays as both a coercive and ideological force in the construction of race" (202).

A work that contemplates whiteness within the area of American literature is Toni Morrison's provocative study *Playing in the Dark: Whiteness and the American Literary Imagination* (1992). In ascertaining the effect on American creativity of what she terms an *Africanist* presence, Morrison investigates "the impact of notions of racial hierarchy, racial exclusion, and racial vulnerability and availability on nonblacks who held, resisted, explored, or altered those notions" (11). She suggests that literary representations of white American identity, as well as American literary form, were fashioned in response to nonwhiteness, specifically the appearance, culture, history, and legal status of African Americans. Morrison's work, together with those previously mentioned, contributes to a body of scholarship that seeks to discover the meaning and making of whiteness in American culture.

The resistance to naming white privilege and the scholarly silence that has precluded the analysis of this racial category are the result of whiteness being presumed the norm. In contrast, racial constructs commonly identified as aberrant, exotic, or Other have been named and explored, precisely because being deemed valid in a culture that seeks to marginalize them necessitates articulation and assessment. Thus, the ways in which these race categories are deconstructed, reconstructed, subverted, embedded, elided; the various tropes, dialectics, stereotypes, histories, and representations that appear in American culture; have received a treatment that whiteness has not. Rarely, for example, do we inquire if terms such as *ofay*, *wasp*, *clay eater*, and *mean whites*, operate within our cultural imagination in the same way as their counterparts, *nigger*, *redskin*, *spic*, and *slant-eye* do; rarely do we query how the being and creation of white artists are intertwined; and rarely do we consider that notions thought to have no racial content often do. It can be argued that Innocence, Freedom, and Individualism, concepts frequently used to characterize American culture and commonly deemed universal, are racialized through implicit exclusion. When cultural representations of American Innocence are predominantly figured through Huckleberry Finn or Shirley Temple, they come to embody a race as much as an idea. Similarly, when Freedom and Individuality are personified through Annie Oakley, John Wayne, or Ronald Reagan (as both actor and president), they too become associated with a particular racial group. When such characterizations are consistently repeated over long periods of time, as they have been in the United States, notions having no specific racial content become racialized. This process weds the racial to the universal, allowing the latter to disguise the former.

Part of the difficulty in characterizing whiteness lies with its having no genuine content other than a culturally manufactured one, developed unevenly over a period of time, influenced by and responding to a variety of historical events and social conditions: among them, the need to create a historical past, the need to create national identity, and the need to minimize class warfare. As whiteness evolved in response to these demands, it did so in no linear or orderly fashion, had no single abiding vision that created it, had no single source from which it sprang. It unfolded ad hoc, as a mishmash of elements attuned to an ever-changing American culture. In different periods, a variety of symbols, laws, and institutions have been mobilized to sustain the concept of whiteness, and over time, repeated representations have cemented its identity. At this point it is useful to trace briefly what historical conditions fostered the creation of whiteness in the United States.

•

In early written records, whiteness did not denote a racially privileged people. In fact, much of the descriptive terminology that in later eras would denigrate nonwhite races—references to apes, to barbarianism, to lack of all but an animal intelligence, and to the impact of geography on cognitive ability—was used to characterize those who would later be grouped under the rubric "white." For example, Chinese historians of the Han dynasty in the third century B.C. described a yellow-haired and green-eyed barbarian people "who greatly resemble monkeys from whom they are descended" (Huxley, 267). Usā-mah Ibn Munqidh, Arab chronicler of the Crusades, wrote of the invading *Franj*, "All those who were well-informed about the *Franj* saw them as beasts superior in courage and fighting ardour but in nothing else, just as animals are superior in strength and aggression" (Maalouf, 39).[6] Similarly, Aristotle in his *Politica* and Vitruvius in his books on architecture suggested geography as the cause of the racial inferiority of northern Europeans:

> Those who live in a cold climate and in Europe are full of spirit, but wanting in intelligence and skill; and therefore they retain comparative freedom, but have no political organization, and are incapable of ruling over others. (Aristotle, 291)

> [I]n the cold regions that are far away from the south, the moisture is not drawn out by hot weather, but the atmosphere is full of dampness which diffuses moisture into the system. . . . This is . . . the reason why the races that are bred in the north are of vast height, and have fair complexions, straight red hair, grey eyes, and a great deal of blood, owing to the abundance of moisture and the coolness of the atmosphere. . . . [T]heir wealth of blood enables them to stand up against the sword without ti-

midity. . . . [N]orthern nations, being enveloped in a dense atmosphere, and chilled by moisture from the obstructing air, have but a sluggish intelligence. (Vitruvius, 170–73)

The absence of a privileged white norm is evident as well in chronicles of early European exploration. Often used to examine European impressions of Africans and of the indigenous populations of the Americas, these documents also offer an opportunity to view the preexistence of whiteness. Those selections from geographer and historian Hakluyt's *Navigations* (1598–1600) devoted to English discovery of other white Europeans indicate geography to be the primary marker of difference and shared appearance to be of minimal importance. This description of Norway after the conquest of King Arthur is an instance: "These people were wild and savage, and had not in them the love of God nor of their neighbors, because all evil commeth from the North" (6–7). In a time when nation-states were still in their nascency, in a time of constant conquest, the tenacious need to characterize what sociologist Franklin H. Giddings would term "consciousness of kind" manifested itself through identification with place rather than identification with appearance. At this early moment, whiteness was not a single racial identity, and tribes of whites were still characterized as English, Norse, or *Franj*.

The Age of Exploration brought with it a solidification of white racial identity. Contact between dissimilar peoples heightened awareness of difference, and in some instances, human variety was warmly embraced. This 1555 Spanish chronicle by Francisco López de Gómara reveals the impact of diverse human appearance on one early observer: "One of the marveylous thynges that god useth in the composition of man, is coloure: whiche doubtlesse can not bee consydered withowte great admiration in beholding one to be white and an other blacke. . . . Sum lykewyse to be yelowe whiche is betwene blacke and white: and other of other colours as it were of dyvers liveres" (Arber, 338). The tolerance and appreciation de Gómara expressed were short lived, however. As nations such as England, Spain, and Portugal became dominant imperialist and colonialist powers, they cemented their own nationalist identities, and in the process, cast their appearance as the human norm, even the human ideal. That the spoils of the European merchant trade began to include Africans and Indians along with cloth and spices facilitated perceptions of non-Europeans as commodities and lesser beings, and increasingly, the linking of countenance to moral character, cognitive capability, and social status strengthened European belief that true humanity had a European aspect.[7]

Once exploration had fostered colonization, attitudes toward racial difference bred practices that further solidified group identity along racial rather than geographic or nationalistic lines. In what would later be the United States, English conviction of their own racial and cultural superiority made the transition from *English* settlers to *white* colonists inevitable. The course of this transition was gradual, however. In *White over Black* (1968), Winthrop Jordan observes:

When Englishmen crossed the Atlantic to settle in America, they were immediately subject to novel strains. In some settlements, notably Jamestown and Plymouth, the survival of the community was in question. An appalling proportion of people were dead within a year, from malnutrition, starvation, unconquerable diseases, bitter cold, oppressive heat, Indian attacks, murder, and suicide. The survivors were isolated from the world as they had known it, cut off from friends and family and the familiar sights and sounds and smells which have always told men who and where they are. . . . For Englishmen planting in America, then, it was of the utmost importance to know that they were Englishmen, which was to say that they were educated (to a degree suitable to their station), Christian (of an appropriate Protestant variety), civilized, and (again to an appropriate degree) free men. (45–46)

Jordan's characterization of these settlers as *English*, *Christian*, and *free*, adjectives that demark nation, religion, and social status, makes no specific reference to whiteness. In this sense, it accurately reflects this clan's view that religion and the need to establish settlement were the preeminent factors unifying them, and not necessarily race—not yet.

Another work that reveals how the English viewed themselves and their endeavor is a propaganda document produced in 1610 by the Virginia Company of London.[8] In *A True and sincere declaration of the purpose and ends of the Plantation begun in Virginia*, religious terms rather than racial ones encourage and justify the colonial mission: "The *Principal* and *Maine Endes* . . . were *first* to preach and baptize into *Christian Religion*, and by propagation of the *Gospell*, to recover out of the armes of the Divell, a number of poore and miserable soules, wrapt up unto death, in almost *invincible ignorance*; . . . and to add our myte to the Treasury of Heaven" (Brown, 339). Rather than differentiate between themselves as white and others as not white, early settlers discriminated between Christians and heathens. The cloistered nature of their society, however, along with their belief that it was their duty to convert others to their religion, produced a fertile environment for the gradual evolution of a racial separateness.

As the colonists' expansionist imperative necessitated the taking of Native American land, and as an increasing slave presence became part of colonial culture, the Christian/heathen distinction changes to a civilized/savage and, subsequently, to a white/nonwhite distinction. The mutability of terms betokening whiteness in early American documents reflects the gradual creation of a racial consciousness capable of justifying acts of conquest as religious and racial rights. A report sent by the Virginia colonists to London after a bloody 1622 confrontation with the Native American leader Opechancanough and the Powhatans reveals a marked shift in perspective from the earlier Virginia Company document: "[O]ur hands, which before were tied with gentleness and fair usage, are now set at liberty by the treacherous violence of the savages . . . the way of conquering them is much more easy than of civilizing them" (qtd. in Gossett, 20). The tone here captures the increasing violence resulting from differing aims, as one people sought to secure land and spread their religion and another sought to maintain their land and religious practices. Settlement by a chosen people converting infidels to God's way became one race's desire to establish dominance by eradication of another, if necessary.

The more English settlers came to see themselves as the rightful heirs of the New World, the more they also saw themselves not just as religious emissaries but as a group united by whiteness. By 1705 the following Virginia code, designed to determine who could or could not own slaves, clearly made apparent the distinction between whites and all others, even if those others were Christians:

> *Be it also enacted, by the authority aforesaid, and it is hereby enacted,* That no negros, mulattos, or Indians, although christians, or Jews, Moors, Mahometans, or other infidels, shall, at any time, purchase any christian servant, nor any other, except of their own complexion, or such as are declared slaves by this act. (Hening, 3:449–50)

The terminology of this statute is revealing. In addition to specifically racializing freedom, its nomenclature reveals the variety of races, religions, and ethnicities that constituted the colonial populace, a diversity that the settlers' language would soon erase. It also reveals that the category "white" is a variable entity, empowered to exclude not only along lines of race, as the references to Africans, Moors, and Native Americans indicate, but also along lines of religion, as the references to Jews and Muslims indicate, and along lines of caste, as the references to slave and servant indicate. From the varying explicit and implicit meanings of *white*, in this passage, it is evident that while the term gained a greater consistency of use and replaced *English, free* and *Christian* as a denotation of the colonists' identity, precisely what *white* embodied—race, religion, class, all of these—was still very much in flux, and it continued to be so into the eighteenth century.

The seventeenth century in the New World saw separation from an established civilization and from ancient tribal identities, and the eighteenth saw unprecedented swells of settlement and land appropriation resulting in a highly mobile and varied population. Between 1760 and 1776 alone, 283 new towns were established in the New England area.[9] The draw to the New World at this time was particularly strong for emigrants from Scotland, Ireland, and England, who for various reasons—obscene land rents and desire to better their lives, for example—sought to migrate to a land of settlers who shared common cultures and common languages. Because modern American culture generally lumps many white ethnicities into one, it is difficult to imagine a time when there was a great deal of fragmentation among whites. By the 1700s, however, the white colonial population consisted of English, Scots, Irish, and, within each of these groups, many heterogenous communities—Scots from the Highlands and Scots from the Hebrides, for example. All were part of a disunified polyglot, divided along lines of ethnicity and class, that had not yet cemented itself into a single white race.

Divisiveness among these groups was common, and at times, ethnic hierarchies exhibited likenesses to prevalent racial ones.

Language in a 1651 letter to Lord General Cromwell from John Cotton, for example, elides the distinctions in social status between Scottish prisoners of war brought to the colonies and Africans brought for servitude or perpetual enslavement:

> The Scots, whom God delivered into your hand at Dunbarre
> . . . we have been desirous (as we could) to make their yoke easy.
> . . . They have not been sold for slaves to perpetuall servitude,
> but for 6 or 7 or 8 yeares, as we do our owne. (Whitmore and
> Appleton, 264–65)

Cotton's comments reveal that, though members of a white race, the Scottish were not members of the ruling ethnic elite and as such were poised between two social identities: servant (generally reserved for whites) and slave for life (generally reserved for Africans). Their skin color carried no guaranteed privilege but allowed the English to view them as being more akin to their "owne," thereby absolving them from lifetime slavery although subjecting them to caste stratification.[10] A similar hierarchizing of white ethnicities is evident in another letter of the period. Christopher Jeaffreson, a prominent English planter in St. Christopher (now St. Kitts), wrote in 1682, "Scotchmen and Welchmen we esteem the best servants; and the Irish the worst, many of them being good for nothing but mischief" (Higham, 169). Both Cotton and Jeaffreson reveal a sensibility not greatly repulsed by white servitude because there was no "consciousness of kind." They did not see the English and other white ethnics as wholly of the same race. Repugnance toward white bondage would increase in direct proportion to the solidification of white racial identity, however, as the experience of indentured servants migrating to the colonies shows. Their history illuminates both the initial lack of a common white consciousness and reasons for its subsequent development.

Generally, indentured servants sold their labor for a period of four to eight years, at the end of which time they were released from obligations and in many cases were given "freedom dues," the money or tools to help establish themselves.[11] Numerous works chronicle their experience, and many of these demonstrate a striking incidence of metaphors evoking portraits of African slavery, as is exemplified in the term *freedom dues*. My intent in investigating the many parallels between servitude and slavery in these writings is not to compare oppressions or to minimize the historical suffering of any people, but rather to depict a time in American history when the social privilege automatically guaranteed to a white skin was still under construction.

One white indentee, James Revel, portrayed his experiences in a poem in which he likened his existence to that of a slave. His reflections reveal an era when the term *slave* was not completely racialized and used to denote solely those of African descent:

> And after sailing seven Weeks and more,
> We at Virginia all were put on shore.
>   Where, to refresh us, we were wash'd and cleaned
> That to our buyers we might better seem;
>   . . . .

And in short time some men up to us came,
. . . .

   Some view'd our limbs, and other's turn'd us round
Examening [!] like Horses, if we're sound,
. . . .

   My fellow slaves were just five Transports more,
With eighteen Negroes, which is twenty four:
. . . .

   We and the Negroes both alike did fare,
Of work and food we had an equal share;
. . . .

Six days we slave for our master's good,
The seventh day is to produce our food. (189–191)

Revel's reference to himself and other white indentees as slaves shows little perception of difference between his lot and that of the African Americans who were part of his transport group. His recollections of being inspected at auction like chattel and being bought by a master resonate with images and terminology that would be used in the genre of the African American slave narrative. An English merchant also blurred the distinction between slave and indentured servant when he commented, "that he could make more money of [white indentured mechanics] than he could of double a quantity of blacks from the coast of Guinea" (*York Courant*, November 23, 1773; qtd. in Bailyn, 301–2). Even in more lighthearted veins this blurring of the two groups is evident. In a London theatrical farce, when a plot to force indenture is revealed, one character exclaims to another, "You kidnapping rascal . . . you was going to send me

into the other world to be turn'd into a black negro" (Joseph Reed, "The Register Office," in *Cawthorn's Minor British Theater* [1806] 3: 43, 53; qtd. in Bailyn, 299). In this example, *slave*, a term used also to refer to white indentured servants, is replaced with *black negro*, an indication of the growing racialization of the "slave" caste that took place in the last quarter of the eighteenth century. Prior to this time, however, the line between the white and the black slave was an unstable one.

To read the many documents describing or decrying the institution of indentured servitude is to read tracts very much akin to the discourse of slavery and abolitionism. A description of the common arrangements for shipping white indentured laborers to the New World reveals how humans were stocked in tiers on boats, as were other commodities:

> Their ships were small—most were between 100 and 300 tons—and the steerage area in which the indentured servants traveled consisted usually of the 'tween decks, or upper hold, space that was used for freight on the inbound voyage. Hogsheads of tobacco and boxes, bags, and crates of other goods were unloaded from the 'tween decks area, which usually had head space of barely 5 feet . . . and wooden slabs, often in two or three tiers, were substituted, to create a tightly jammed, airless dormitory. (Bailyn, 316)

Another trader, William Stevenson, had "gratings and air ports" cut in one of his ships, following the pattern of African slavers that had no forced ventilation because the owners "endeavor to give [the slaves] a more equal and moderate current of air" (William Stevenson to James Cheston, Bristol, April 9,

1768, James Cheston, Incoming Letters [1767–1782], boxes 9-15, Cheston Galloway Papers, M-1650, Maryland Hall of Records, Annapolis; qtd. in Bailyn, 318–319).

On arrival in the colonies, indentured servants were arranged for "sale." Most were dispatched at port auctions, and those not "sold" at port were engaged to employers through the process of extended sales, traveling backcountry secondary markets until they were engaged. On viewing one auction, Frederick Schmidt, a London weaver, used references to African enslavement to express his repulsion to the spectacle of white human bondage:

> They all was sett in a row . . . near a hundred man & women & the planter come down the cuntry to buy. . . . I never see such pasels or pore raches [wretches] in my lif som all most naked and what had cloths was as black as chimney swipers, and all most starved by the ill usidge in ther pasedge by the capn, for they are used no bater than so many negro slaves that are brought in hare and sold in the same manner as horss or cows in our market or fair. ("British Convict Servant Labor in Colonial Virginia." Ph.D. Diss., College of William and Mary, 1976, 156; qtd. in Bailyn, 326)

The difference in tone and language between Stevenson's letter and Schmidt's observations is instructive. In the first, an educated merchant secure in his social position looks dispassionately upon the conscription of whites for servitude. In the second, a tradesman having no formal education and not far removed from the social strata from which many of the indentured class originated is far more empathetic. While both evoke the specter of African slaves, Stevenson's is a matter-of-fact comparison, pragmatically considering the best way to ship human cargo. Schmidt's analogy, in contrast, expresses disgust that whites should be treated as "negro slaves" and foreshadows the distance white skin would subsequently place between white servants and black slaves-for-life. More important, however, the class insecurity implied in Schmidt's words suggests why de-emphasizing their own national and cultural identities to take advantage of the caste protection offered by white skin appealed to many migrating Europeans of the laboring classes.

Being shipped as cargo, sold at auction, advertised as runaways, and prevented from full political participation because they owned no property made slavery and disenfranchisement more than a metaphor for many indentured whites, and seeking any means to ensure that they did not slide from the tenuous caste of servant into the permanent caste of slave-for-life was imperative. The Irish, for example, had a concrete history of coerced bondage and separation of families that vivified the experience of slavery. According to Theodore Allen, from 1652 to 1657,

> [U]pon application to the English authorities, merchants were issued licenses to take cargoes of Irish to America for sale as bond-laborers. . . . Subsequently the common practice was direct negotiation between the slave trader and the magistrates, jail-keepers and overseers of the poor in specific Irish localities. The procedure was conducted under color of the English va-

grancy act of 1597. . . . Nevertheless, it served just as well for capturing, selling and transporting non-vagrants, as actual vagrants. (74)

That more than half the investors in Irish plantations such as Ulster were also stockholders in the Virginia Company; that many Irish were captured and forced to migrate to the United States and, in the process, were separated from family; and that many were forced to renew contracts for multiple periods suggests a continuum of enslavement in which appearance offered little relief.[12]

The tenuous position of indentured servants is further illustrated in the following 1672 statute crafted essentially to deter unity among the dispossessed:

> FORASMUCH as it hath beene manifested to this grand assembly that many negroes have lately beene, and now are out in rebellion in sundry parts of this country, and that noe meanes have yet beene found for the apprehension and suppression of them from whome many mischeifes of very dangerous consequence may arise to the country if either other negroes, Indians or servants should happen to fly forth and joyne with them; for the prevention of which, *Be it enacted by the governour, councell and burgesses of this grand assembly, and by the authority theoreof,* that if any negroe, molatto, Indian slave, or servant for life, runaway and shalbe persued by warrant or hue and crye, it shall and may be lawfull for any person who shall endeavor to take them, upon the resistance of such negroe, molatto, Indian slave, or servant for life, to kill or wound him or them soe resisting. (Hening, 2: 299)

The statute makes minimal distinctions among the social status terms *negroes, Indians, servants, molatto* (mulatto), *Indian slave,* and *servant for life*; and the blurring of these categories does not afford impoverished whites any special protection from being treated as others of the disenfranchised classes. It is understandable, then, that these whites would embrace any guise that guaranteed even the most nominal freedom and prestige, and being classified as white provided one.

Being white may have secured a social status distinct from enslaved blacks or displaced Native Americans, but it did not necessarily confer full social acceptance in an emerging republic whose nationalistic origins were English. As the colonies merged into a nation, discussion of how national identity would be classified intensified, and those framing the debate questioned who had the right to call themselves American and thereby enjoy the full privileges of that title. Was national identity to embody solely planters and merchants of English stock; the white indentured servants from other European ethnicities, so necessary to the rapid settlement and development of the colonies; the original Native American inhabitants of the land; the descendants of Africans imported by the slave trade? For John Jay, the answer was simple. Ignoring the plurality of colonial America, he envisioned the new nation as a white nation:

> It has often given me pleasure to observe, that independent America was not composed of detached and distant territories, but that one connected, fertile, wide-spreading country was the portion of our western sons of liberty. . . .

With equal pleasure I have as often taken notice, that Providence has been pleased to give this one connected country to one united people—a people descended from the same ancestors, speaking the same language, professing the same religion, attached to the same principles of government, very similar in their manners and customs. (*The Federalist* No. 2, in Hamilton, Jay, and Madison, 8–9)

Unlike Jay, Benjamin Franklin found grappling with a variety of races and ethnicities while conceptualizing the national identity more problematic. In "Observations Concerning the Increase of Mankind," he seems to advocate the establishment of a white state when he queries, "why increase the Sons of Africa, by Planting them in America, where we have so fair an Opportunity, by excluding all Blacks and Tawneys, of increasing the lovely White and Red?" (Labaree, 234), but later reveals that his desire to eradicate "Blacks and Tawneys" extends to other white ethnics as well. In the same piece, while contemplating increasing German immigration to Pennsylvania, he contends:

[W]hy should the Palatine Boors be suffered to swarm into our Settlements, and by herding together establish their Language and Manners to the Exclusion of ours? Why should Pennsylvania, founded by the English, become a Colony of *Aliens*, who will shortly be so numerous as to Germanize us instead of our Anglifying them, and will never adopt our Language or Customs, any more than they can acquire our Complexion. (Labaree, 234)

For Franklin, clearly, the English had a different complexion from the Germans and even from the French, Russians, and Swedes. He concludes:

> [T]he Number of purely white People in the World is proportionably very small. All Africa is black or tawny. Asia chiefly tawny. America (exclusive of the new Comers) wholly so. And in Europe, the Spaniards, Italians, French, Russians and Swedes, are generally of what we call a swarthy Complexion; as are the Germans also, the Saxons only excepted, who with the English, make the principal Body of White People on the Face of the Earth. I could wish their Numbers were increased. (Labaree, 234)

Like Jay, Franklin envisioned the United States as a white nation, "wholly so"; but Franklin is considerably more specific than his compatriot. His observations establish a clear hierarchy in which English is the preferred form of white, a hierarchy that would influence the fate of subsequent generations of whites. Franklin thus recasts the notion of *complexion*, enabling it to denote cultural and national affiliation—English—rather than physical attributes. By so doing he echoes earlier chroniclers who used means of classification other than physical appearance. The writings of Franklin and Jay display, through political discourse, the tenuous nature of group racial identity among a fragmented white populace. Exhibiting the same sentiments in the discourse of travel narrative are an interesting pair of documents authored by William Byrd.

In 1728, Byrd was part of a surveying team sent to map the border between Virginia and North Carolina. During his sojourn, he wrote a set of diaries of his experience, one an immediate record of the journey titled *The Secret History of the Dividing Line Betwixt Virginia and North Carolina* and the other a more official version titled *The History of the Dividing Line Betwixt Virginia and North Carolina*. The difference between the two versions is instructive. Scholars generally agree that the *Secret History* represents Byrd's immediate recollections and responses and that the *History* is the version that was edited for public consumption, one that scaled down gossip and the divulging of the crew's sexual escapades and rendered in more detail the topography and the process of surveying.[13] In essence, Byrd's documents can be viewed as indigenous travel narratives, the product of an aristocratic explorer giving his impressions of life outside his "civilization." Not unlike other travel writers, Byrd sought to give his readers a visceral sense of the woods and swamps of North Carolina and Virginia and thus rendered in great detail both topography and the "exotic" Others he met on the way. In his case, however, the Other is not African, Chinese, Latina(o) or Indian but rather the Otherly white.[14]

Byrd's descriptions disclose sentiments of contempt for whites outside his class and English ethnicity. The passages below, taken from both versions of Byrd's writing, detail an encounter with a North Carolina backwoodsman. From the *Secret History*:

Meanwell and I made a Visit to Cornelius Keath, who liv'd rather in a Penn than a House, with his Wife and 6 Children. I never beheld such a Scene of Poverty in this happy part of the World. The Hovel they lay in had no Roof to cover those wretches from the Injurys of the Weather: but when it rain'd, or was colder than Ordinary, the whole Family took refuge in a Fodder Stack. The poor man had rais'd a kind of a House but for want of Nails it remain'd uncover'd. . . . The man can read & write very well, and by way of a Trade can make & set up Quernstones[15] & yet is poorer than any Highland-Scot, or Bog-trotting Irishman. (305)

From the *History*:

We landed at the Plantation of Cornelius Keith, where I beheld the wretchedest Scene of Poverty I had ever met with in this happy Part of the World. The Man, his Wife and Six Small Children, liv'd in a Penn, like so many Cattle, without any Roof over their Heads but that of Heaven. And this was their airy Residence in the Day time, but then there was a Fodder Stack not far from this Inclosure, in which the whole Family shelter'd themselves a night's and in bad weather.

However, 'twas almost worth while to be as poor as this Man was, to be as perfectly contented. All his Wants proceeded from Indolence, and not from Misfortune. He had good Land, as well as good Health and good Limbs to work it, and, besides, had a Trade very useful to all the Inhabitants round about. He cou'd make and set up Quern Stones very well, and had proper Materials for that purpose just at Hand, if he cou'd have taken the pains to fetch them. . . .

> I am sorry to say it, but Idleness is the general character of
> the men in the Southern Parts of this Colony as well as in North
> Carolina. The Air is so mild, and the Soil so fruitful, that very
> little Labour is requir'd to fill their Bellies, especially where the
> Woods afford such Plenty of Game. (304)

Since Byrd was consciously rendering a public document, one that he took care to augment for posterity, he no doubt was very aware of the tone of his words. It is significant that the first version of the *Histories* contains what might be tantamount to "racial" slurs—the references to a "Highland-Scot" and a "Bog-trotting Irishman"—and that the version doctored for public consumption does not. What is evident in Byrd's public/private split is a strongly tribal identity, located in an English self and contemptuous of whites outside his group, and a second identity aware of its place in history and resorting not to ethnic differentiation to explain differences among whites but to pseudoscientific explanations such as climate ("I am sorry to say it, but Idleness is the general character of the men in the Southern Parts of this Colony"). Byrd's writing suggests that, for a writer of this time, whiteness as a racial appearance alone did not signal any type of conscious unity, any presumption that common appearance signified common values, economic class, aspirations, and thoughts. The separation that Byrd implicitly placed between his own social identity and that of the North Carolina backwoodspeople portrays a point in American culture when the white identity was still relatively unstable and undefined.

Though group identity among white ethnics remained factional, and though ethnic identification remained, heterogeneous European communities increasingly would coalesce into a white race that viewed itself as prototypically American. As early as 1782, Hector Crèvecoeur defined the American as "either an European, or the descendant of an European" (49). He could do so because whiteness, an imagined, created category, had fashioned a dominant American racial group out of a European patchwork quilt. It cemented varied white European populations into a unified nation-state and located social power in one group.

From the 1700s on, whiteness is key to the maintenance of American nation-state identity. It replaced a cohesive Old World culture whose beliefs, traditions, and practices bound a people together over time. It assuaged the worries of cultural loss articulated by Samuel Johnson in his 1773 tour of Scotland: "[A] nation scattered in the boundless regions of *America* resembles rays diverging from a focus. All the rays remain, but the heat is gone. Their power consisted in their concentration: when they are dispersed, they have no effect" (109). Whiteness retained the "heat" of an unsettled, migrating people, grounding them, giving permanence and commonality of identity. To the different ethnicities and classes who left Europe to come to an unfamiliar wilderness where new structures had to be devised to meet new needs, whiteness furnished a social order that forged a nascent national identity and minimized potential class warfare.

Essential to the making of an exclusive white national identity was the construction of an imagined past that would enable a variety of whites to conceive a common heritage. The manufacture of a white racial antecedent, as opposed to an English, Irish, Welsh, or Scottish one, provided a common ancestry for a nation of white ethnics that had become a race, as well as a rationale for excluding nonwhites from full participation in the new nation. Fabricated beginnings gave whiteness rituals, content, and meaning that allowed it to respond to rapid social transformations, such as the transition from colonies to states to nation, the social upheavals of constant migrations, the advent of industrial capitalism, and the disruption of social patterns caused by many racial and religious groups challenging configurations of power and authority along racial, religious, and gender lines.

Certainly, English origins contributed to fashioning a racial past for whiteness, but its historical content derived more from imagined legacies than actual ones. In particular, the white consciousness fancied Teutonic and Anglo-Saxon antecedents as its genesis. In the eighteenth and nineteenth centuries, the character and practices of northern European Germanic tribes were mythologized, adapted, and adopted to serve the needs of particular eras in American history. In *Race: The History of an Idea in America* (1963) Thomas F. Gossett suggests that Teutonic origins theories, so popular in the eighteenth century, held a particular attraction to the American psyche of this time because many of the principles of Teuton organization could be superimposed on concepts of American representative government.[16] Teutonic rule by *witenagenot* (a council) as opposed to centralized monarchies seemed an ancestral manifestation of the newly created forms of government emerging in the United States. For many defenders of these new systems, drawing similarities between Teutonic government and emerging American democracy cemented an ancient, non-English sovereignty to a new one seeking through its revolution to distinguish itself from English traditions. Concomitantly, the identification with a Teutonic past effectively racialized and gendered American governance, making it by ancestral rights the property of white men in the United States, who could, at their discretion, determine who would or would not be participating members.

Of greater appeal than similarity in forms of governance, however, were the character traits attributed to Germanic people. Conceptions of this group were loosely based on the ancient writings of Tacitus, who characterized Germanic tribes in the following manner:

[T]he peoples of Germany have not been polluted by any marriages with other tribes and . . . they have existed as a particular people, pure and only like themselves. As a result, all have the same bodily appearance, as far as is possible in so large a number of men: fiery blue eyes, red hair, large bodies which are strong only for violent exertion. (65)

[M]any noble young men of their own accord seek those tribes which are then waging some war, since quiet is displeasing to the race and they become famous more easily in the midst of dangers. (70)

These qualities of race purity and desire for conquest suited well the imagination of a nation bent on expanding its boundaries to the north, south, and west and would influence conceptions of whiteness into the twentieth century. They allowed white Americans to see themselves as a pure race whose noble qualities of superior beauty, intellect, initiative, and ability to conquer and govern had been concentrated through avoidance of dilution by inferior racial stock.

The 1893 writings of Columbia University political scientist John Burgess reveal how closely an imagined Teutonic past was joined to the mission of nineteenth-century American manifest destiny:

> The civilized states have a claim upon the uncivilized populations, as well as a duty towards them, and that claim is that they shall become civilized. . . . If the barbaric populations resist the same, *à l'outrance*, the civilized state may clear the territory of their presence and make it the abode of civilized man. . . . The fact that a politically unorganized population roves through a wilderness, or camps within it, does not create rights, either public or private, which a civilized state, pursuing its great world-mission, is under any obligations, legal or moral, to respect. . . . History and ethnology offer us this elevated ground, and they teach us that the Teutonic nations are the political nations of the modern era. (46–48)

In 1845, Congressman Alexander Duncan, representative of Ohio, expressed similar sentiments far more naïvely, when he credited Anglo-Saxon qualities as the source of a stable American democracy. In the 1840s debate surrounding the annexation of Texas and Oregon, Duncan commented, "Providence seems to have a design in extending our free institutions as far and as wide as the American continent. . . . Wherever our settlements have been pushed and our laws have been extended, all that have existed of human laws and of human beings have given way. There seems to be something in our laws and institutions peculiarly adapted to our Anglo-Saxon-American race, under which they will thrive and prosper, but under which all others wilt and die" (178). In his 1845 bill, Duncan conveniently avoided consideration of how removals and enslavement facilitated the wilting and dying he saw as a providential result of Anglo-Saxon heritage.[17]

Creating Teutonic, Anglo-Saxon, or, as in the early twentieth century, Nordic origins satisfied a desire for racial history and antecedents, even if this imagined past was in direct conflict with the multiple ethnicities, languages, physical appearances, cultures, and class statuses that formed the actuality of American existence.[18] An ancestral underpinning made whiteness seem an ancient group identity to which any white, regardless of class or ethnicity, could belong. Whiteness was thus able to function as a unifying device, diffusing class warfare among whites while continually integrating new white immigrants into the white American fabric. Further, by establishing itself as a naturally superior racial identity, whiteness reconciled such undemocratic practices as full social enfranchisement only for some, enslavement, forced removal, and internment with democratic ideals.

Once conceived, whiteness maintained itself hegemonically. Philosopher Antonio Gramsci's observations on the functions of social hegemony assist in conceptualizing how this process occurs. Gramsci outlines the sources of hegemony, and thus the prerequisites necessary to the sustenance of whiteness, as follows:

> 1. The "spontaneous" consent given by the great masses of the population to the general direction imposed on social life by the dominant fundamental group; this consent is "historically" caused by the prestige (and consequent confidence) which the dominant group enjoys because of its position and function in the world of production.
>
> 2. The apparatus of state coercive power which "legally" enforces discipline on those groups who do not "consent" either actively or passively. This apparatus is, however, constituted for the whole of society in anticipation of moments of crisis of command and direction when spontaneous consent has failed. (12)

Gramsci's explanations create a framework for understanding how whiteness is imbued with privileged authority through political, economic, and cultural means. Restricting who can vote, own property,[19] or serve on juries; inhibiting access to the means of capitalistic production; filling cultural institutions with representations only of whites and allowing those images to dominate literary, visual, and performing arts all generate a spontaneous, if subconscious, recognition of the supremacy of whiteness and sanction the perception that whites intrinsically have more right to what is American than do other groups in the United States.

The devices employed in creating white hegemony are for the most part devices of exclusion. They articulate not necessarily who or what is white but rather who or what is not white. As such, they reveal the fundamental paradox of whiteness: the persistent need of nonwhiteness to give it form and expression. The very existence of whiteness embodies an odd duality of distinguishing itself from something nonwhite while appropriating the nonwhite to justify its being and, at a later stage in its development, its unique Americanness. The colonists were best able to vindicate their claim to the New World by conceiving of themselves as a chosen white people and using difference from Native Americans and Africans to concretize that identity. Indentured servants were best able to define themselves as enfranchised citizens by distinguishing their status from that of black slaves-for-life. European immigrant laborers became white and, through contention with a nonwhite populace, elevated their social prestige if at the expense of their own economic benefit. This pattern of denial and appropriation is also evident in cultural creations, particularly literature, where writers who claimed themselves white could create an indigenous American literature only by adopting or responding to the dialect, imagery, characterizations, and creations of nonwhites. The novels *The Last of the Mohicans* (1826) and *Huckleberry Finn* (1884/5), both credited with breaking American imitation of English forms and content, could not have done so without depending largely on Native American and African American elements. A permanent "twoness" thus emerges within white American identity, characterized by the desire to claim racial purity while ignoring the cultural blending and appropriation that are inextricably part of its form.

It would be convenient to define whiteness as a biological classification, a class rank, or an indicator of common consciousness; but its development in the United States indicates that it is none of these and yet all of these. The history of African Americans who passed for white while living in constant fear of discovery reminds us that whiteness cannot be defined only in terms of physical appearance. The treatment of white laborers at the hands of a landed or industrial elite reminds us that white privilege sometimes disappears in the face of class interest. English resistance to immigrants from nations as varied as Germany, Sweden, France, and Russia recalls that whiteness does not always produce a consciousness of kind. What the history of whiteness in the United States reveals is that we need to enlarge our conception of what whiteness is. It is larger than having the physical attribute of white skin; it is the ideology that was created around that attribute.

The ideology of whiteness asserts that those with white skin are more deserving of employment, sound housing, quality education, and equitable social treatment than those without that attribute. As an ideology, it enlists institutions to support its credos: museums, for example which eternize the artistic and historical visions of white-skinned peoples, or television which even with recent inclusions of nonwhite experience still depicts whiteness as an American norm. The ideology of whiteness influences many areas of social activity, from one's likelihood of successfully hailing a cab, to one's likelihood of shopping without being shadowed by retail security, to one's likelihood of securing a mortgage. Because of the ideology surrounding their appearance, people with white skin from a variety of class and educational backgrounds have, throughout history, formed, enforced, or benignly acquiesced to laws and public policy that have sustained their own racial interests. Certain periods in American cultural history best illuminate the development of an ideology of whiteness: in particular, English settlement and the colonial periods, the nineteenth century, and the beginning of the twentieth century. In these eras, specific cultural dynamics that foster invented icons, laws, institutions, and rituals can be seen imparting a white-race ethos to a pluralistic American culture.

2

Crafting Whiteness
in Early America

Superiores sint, qui superiores esse sciunt.
(Let them be superior who know they are superior.)
—*Cotton Mather*

I BEGIN MANY of my American literature courses with writings
of the prenational period. Students generally grumble, expect-
ing tract after tract of Calvinist proclamations praising the religious inspiration that envisioned the establishment of a new
Canaan on the North American continent. What they do not
expect is the immense diversity of these documents, which include (or should include) written transcriptions of Native
American chronicles; statutes regulating everything from the
treatment of livestock to the interaction of racial, ethnic, and
class groups; religious histories; journals; and travel narratives.
Students are genuinely excited by the many visions of this period, which reveal prenational America to be more of a land
without borders than is commonly thought. For a moment in
history, the close proximity of Europeans, Africans, Native
Americans, and others held the potential for multiple ex-

changes among diverse peoples, which might have served as the foundation for a truly pluralistic democratic vision. Sadly, what this literature also reveals is how this vision was sacrificed to the creation of whiteness.

The period spanning English migration to North America to the establishment of the colonies is one of the most instructive in American cultural history for observing the construction of whiteness as an ideology, a system of beliefs privileging those with white skin. Documents of this early era record the formation of whiteness and how its development shaped perceptions of the varied races, ethnicities, classes, and genders that populated prenational America.[1] Though generally read for their historical content, writings of the colonial period are more than records of deeds; they are annals of the contestations and social values that led to the creation of American whiteness. Over the course of the seventeenth and early eighteenth centuries, they imagined, solidified, and transmitted an increasingly uniform model of this social ideology. In these records the cornerstones for subsequent representations of American white identity were laid.

American whiteness is essentially an English creation, arising in response to migration, encounter, and a need to sustain established social structures in a new environment. English cultural, religious, and political values shaped it, and English travel narratives, journals, histories, and narratives of crime and captivity provide the most extensive formal record of its representations. In these writings an evolution is evident, from documents that colonize an area through the written word, to documents that reflect an English community increasingly defining itself in terms of other races, to documents that begin to fix racial types.

The Cartographers

Early maps and travel narratives were the first accounts to chronicle English impressions of the New World. As they did so, they charted a psychic space within which American whiteness developed. An initial step in this charting was a blending of images and prose that colonized new terrain through printed matter and pictorial representations. Maps foreshadowed visually the ways in which English narrative prose would claim land through words and as such are a fitting prelude to an analysis of accounts of exploration and their relationship to constructions of whiteness.

In addition to being directional guides, maps are material artifacts that represent cultural perceptions during particular periods of history. According to cartologist Mark Monmonier, a map could be an "intellectual tool for legitimizing territorial conquest, economic exploitation, and cultural imperialism. Maps made it easy for European states to carve up Africa and other heathen lands, to lay claim to land and resources, and to ignore existing social and political structures" (90). The figurative conquest outlined by Monmonier is evident in the images that accompany some early European maps. In the 1540s, for example, the New World was drawn as an unknown space, dotted with then-popular representations of the inhabitants and animals encountered during surveys of eastern Europe, Africa, and Asia. One such map, published in 1544 and believed to represent Sebastian Cabot's interpretation of his father John Cabot's travels to North America names the eastern part of this continent "*terra incognita.*" Its visuals depict a primitive, fur-draped people holding spears and a leopard-like animal standing nearby. The portraits of humans and fauna are telling, for they indicate how the European imagination superimposed on a territory it had yet to traverse familiar images inspired by previous exploration (Figure 1). This superimposition was an initial step in the process of settlement, in that it rendered the unknown less so by characterizing an unexplored continent through impressions already associated with European expansionism.

Similar conceptions of the New World are manifest in a 1547 French map credited to cartographer Nicolas Vallard. This map is particularly significant for its revelation of how colonial powers saw themselves in relation to the lands they sought to conquer. A small band of settlers—male and female, gentry and yeomen, religious and secular—stand gathered holding guns and javelins, foregrounded against a large landmass dotted with men in scouts' garb, deer, foxes, dogs, bears, and women and men in bearskins. One colonist points to a group of apparently indigenous people, and in the lower left corner, an indigenous person points to the group of colonists. Both images seem to be gestures of discovery, as each group notes the other's presence (Figure 2).

The progression from the earlier Cabot map to the later one by Vallard reveals a shift in perception, from seeing the land

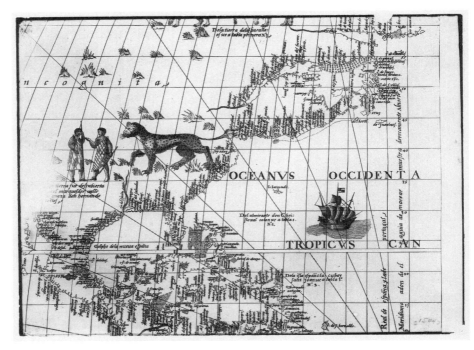

1. This 1544 Cabot map of Eastern North America reveals how 0Europeans imagined the inhabitants and animals of "terra incognita." (LIBRARY OF CONGRESS GEOGRAPHY AND MAP DIVISION READING ROOM)

as inhabited by unknown indigenous elements, made familiar only by their approximation to elements of past discovery, to seeing the land as an area upon which a European presence is becoming situated. In this progression, a growing sense of European entitlement to the Americas is evident, a sense that will be central to later conceptions of whiteness.

An example of the increasingly proprietary English attitude

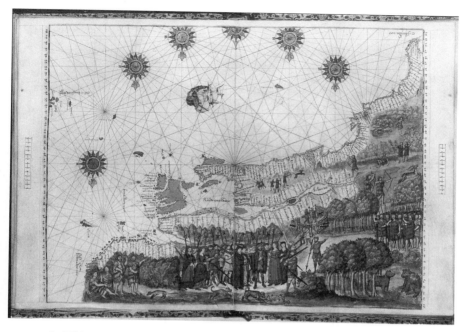

2. This 1547 map of Eastern North America by Nicolas Vallard simulates scenes of "first contact" among indigenous peoples and European settlers. (BY PERMISSION OF THE HUNTINGTON LIBRARY, SAN MARINO, CALIFORNIA)

toward North America is evident in the exploration narratives of John Smith. *A Map of Virginia* (1612), the map that accompanies Smith's account reflects a blend of worlds. At this point, though English elements are present, the North American land area takes up most of the map's space. At the map's bottom center is an ornate scale of leagues and half leagues; in its lower left corner are a compass and a ship sailing what has been termed the "Virginian Sea." On the landmass itself the name

3. *(above)* and 4. *(facing page)* A comparison of Smith's map of Virginia with his map of New England reveals a growing sense of English entitlement to North America. (LIBRARY OF CONGRESS GEOGRAPHY AND MAP DIVISION READING ROOM)

Virginia appears, along with the royal coat of arms and a sizable figure that Smith labels a Susquehannock Native American. In the upper left corner is an illustration of the Native American leader Powhatan and his followers, and indigenous names for rivers and valleys are plentiful (Figure 3). What this map displays is a land that is not yet English, one still the domain of

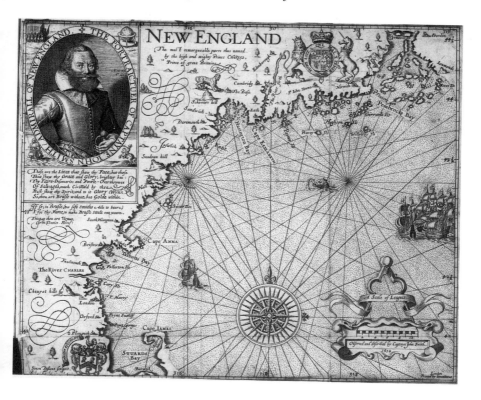

its native peoples. Maps in subsequent Smith works portray growing English imperialism, however.

In a map drafted to accompany *A Description of New England* (1616), Smith's image in the upper left corner of the map dwarfs the land itself. Prominently to the side of Smith's picture is the name New England and the royal coat of arms. Aside from a leopard-like animal and a few trees dotting the landscape, no indigenous elements are present. The names on the map are mostly English, detailing various "discoveries." The English presence here is augmented, shown as one that has both conquered and renamed the New World (Figure 4).

The last of the Smith maps treated here is included in his most well known work, *Generall historie of Virginia* (1624). It represents a notable transition from mapmaking to storytelling, as the English presence in the New World is mythologized through a series of pictures that relate Smith's North American escapades. Resembling a modern comic strip, the map has seven image tiles—three sharing the top row, and four the bottom. The tiles are arranged chronologically and have the following captions: "C. Smith bound to a tree to be shott to death, 1607"; "Their conjuration about C. Smith, 1607"; "C. Smith taketh the King of Pamaunkee prisoner, 1608"; "C. Smith takes the King of Paspahegh prisoner, 1609"; and "King Powhatan commands C. Smith to be slayne, his daughter Pokahantas beggs his life." The middle tile of the bottom row contains a map of "Ould" Virginia with a preponderance of English names and a few native ones. This square is the only nod to an actual map within this sequence of visual events that subordinates cartography to the legend of English conquest (Figure 5).[2]

Smith's narratives, like the maps issued with them, portray the Americas as imminently English. *A Map of Virginia* in particular, through detailed descriptions of climate and land, characterizes North America as an environment fit not just for

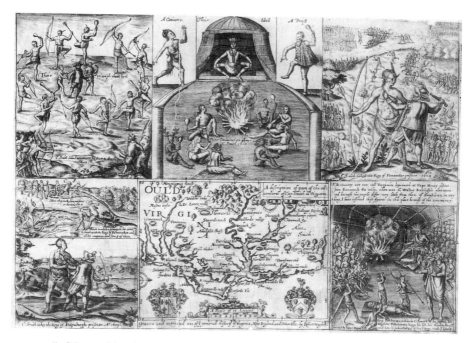

5. Mapmaking becomes subordinated to myth-making in this map
accompanying John Smith, *Generall historie of Virginia.* (LIBRARY OF
CONGRESS GEOGRAPHY AND MAP DIVISION READING ROOM)

settlement but specifically for English settlement: "The country is not mountanous nor yet low but such pleasant plaine hils
& fertle valleyes . . . watered so conveniently with their sweete
brookes and christall springs" (3); "The temperature of this
countrie doth agree well with English constitutions being
once seasoned to the country" (1). As well, Smith further angli-
cized the land through the appropriation that comes with
naming:

The cape on the South-side is called *Cape Henry* in honour of our most noble Prince. The shew of the land there is a white hilly sand like unto the Downes, and along the shores great plentie of Pines and Firres.

The north *Cape* is called *Cape Charles* in honour of the worthy Duke of *Yorke*. Within is a country that may have the prerogative over the most pleasant places of *Europe*, *Asia*, *Africa*, or *America*, for large and pleasant navigable rivers, heaven & earth never agreed better to frame a place for mans habitation being of our constitutions, were it fully manured and inhabited by industrious people. (2)

In noting how areas of an unfamiliar land replicated locations in Europe and were suited to English industry, Smith made a new landscape seem a natural extension of the old. Naming settlements as Cape Charles or Cape Henry after British monarchs provided a connective between old English social structures and the order that would emerge across the Atlantic. Comparing this area to others of English conquest in Africa, Asia, and America suggested a certain inevitability to English control of the North American continent, and Smith's mention of heaven and earth never agreeing "better to frame a place" for "our constitutions" foreshadowed the notion of divine right that the English would employ to justify their enterprise. Overall, Smith's *Map* made the process of settling less daunting by creating written assurance of continuity between old and new and of divine sanction of English efforts.

As well as making unknown terrain familiar, Smith's *Map* lessened the threat posed by unfamiliar peoples. His accounts of Native Americans serve as early ethnography, explaining one people to another. He identified potential commonalities, thus making the attributes and customs of a native populace less alien to his readership. Physical difference between the English and Native Americans, for example, was minimized by the observation that their offspring, to his thinking, were born with "white" appearances: "The people differ very much in stature . . . but generally tall and straight, of a comely proportion, & of a colour browne when they are of any age, but they are borne white" (19). Similarly, when compelled to characterize native religion as idolatrous or as "Divell worship," Smith underscored common ground by noting that "savages," too, have some conception of a divine essence:

> There is yet in *Virginia* no place discovered to bee so *Savage* in which the *Savages* have not a religion. . . . All things that were able to do the[m] hurt beyond their prevention, they adore with their kinde of divine worship; as the fire, water, lightning, thunder, our ordinance, peeces, horses, &c. But their chiefe God they worship is the Divell. Him they call *Oke* & serve him more offeare then love. (29)

What Smith accomplished elsewhere when describing terrain he here accomplished in passages that construct indigenous peoples of North America as at once Other and comprehensible. In both instances, he rendered the fearsome less so, and an initial hindrance to colonization, fear of the unknown, was thus mitigated.

In essence, the sense of entitlement expressed in Smith's accounts accustomed English minds to thinking of the North American continent as theirs for the taking.[3] This proprietary attitude fostered subsequent avowals of English superiority to sustain the belief of English right to North America. As we will see, however, when the advancement of their enterprise became dependent on their casting their lot with those of other white European nationals, assertions of English superiority were replaced by assertions of white superiority.

The Visionaries

The documents of John Smith were not the only early writings to claim the New World as English and eventually pave the way for broader European claims and resultant constructions of whiteness to justify them. Other works did so not by colonizing a landscape through words but by casting colonization as divine providence. The English belief in a divine right to North America was essential to the success of their enterprise; but even more important to the purposes of this work is that this belief became essential in the composition of a myth of American origins that would be crucial to constructing and maintaining whiteness in what later became the United States. The ethos of divine right laid the attitudinal foundation for American whiteness by allowing the English to justify the exclusion from full participation in their sanctioned community of those who were not like them, whether because of religious, national, or racial differences.

Nowhere are perceptions of divinely sanctioned English right to settle the New World more evident than in the written record of New England. As the settlements most able to sustain the trades of printing and bookselling and to attract the elite of the intellectual clergy, the region produced a preponderance of religious writings, journals, and histories that afford the possibility of viewing the values and attitudes that motivated an influential segment of the prenational mind.[4] Puritan authors dominate much of this written record; hence, the account is heavily laden with their overtones, particularly their emphasis on the covenantal relationship between their people and God.[5] Their writings mythologize English experiences, turning migrants into pilgrims sharing a special bond with God as they settle a new land. The literature also documents the lessening prominence of religious leadership in a community increasingly defining itself in secular terms. Noticeable in this transition is the growing use of whiteness to represent English social identity. Because of an absence of concrete European nationalistic borders, because of land contestations with Native Americans, and because of increasingly intimate cohabitation with African servants and slaves, less visible differences of class, religion, and ethnicity become subordinate to the more visible difference of physical appearance. Two of New England's most prominent chroniclers, both Puritan, provide an ideal theater for viewing the evolution from religious and ethnic self-definition to racial self-definition.[6]

One of the earliest documents of Puritan experience in the New World is *Of Plymouth Plantation* (1620–1647) written by the colony's subsequent governor William Bradford. It is here, according to David Levin, "that we read of 'pilgrims' who obey their calling to leave the known European world for a wilderness, seeking comfort in the Biblical reminder that heaven is their dearest country" (in Emerson, 12). Bradford's record of his pilgrims' progress is transformed into an American origins myth, variously told and retold in later literature, and from the outset, it is evident that separateness and difference are key components of this myth.[7]

Bradford's history begins prior to English arrival on American shores, and in his descriptions of the Puritan sojourn in the Netherlands before voyaging west, the insularity of a religious community that views all others as outsiders, even those sharing the same physical appearance, is apparent:

> Being now come into the Low Countries, they . . . heard a strange and uncouth language, and beheld the different manners and customs of the people, with their strange fashions and attires; all so far differing from that of their plain country villages (wherein they were bred and had so long lived) as it seemed they were come into a new world.[8] (16)

The cloisteredness portrayed in Bradford's narrative transferred itself to the actual New World, where it was tested by contact with other religious, ethnic, and racial groups and where it would resist contamination from outsiders by constantly articulating definitions of its separateness. One means it would use to maintain lines of separation was the characterization of other peoples of the North American continent in ways that were clearly meant to privilege Puritan identity. Bradford's early perceptions of Native Americans, which evolved into popular racial representations, are an illustration.

In imagining the New World and its inhabitants, Bradford wrote the following:

> The place they had thoughts on was some of those vast and *unpeopled* countries of America, which are fruitful and fit for habitation, being devoid of all *civil* inhabitants, where there are only *savage* and *brutish* men which range up and down, little otherwise than the *wild beasts* of the same. (26; italics mine)

Though the characterization of Native Americans as uncivil, "savage," "wild beasts" abates in subsequent passages, where Bradford named those he came in contact with first as "Indians" and then, more specifically, as "Narragansett," "Mohegan," and "Pequot," his early descriptions reflect the race content the New England imagination employed as it began to distinguish its identity from that of another people. In this instance, conceiving of Native Americans as savage allowed English Puritans to formulate a group identity in which they were "not-savage."[9] New England consisted of more than just English Puritans, however, and also apparent in Bradford's chronicle are those tensions that make forming group identity a complex undertaking.

The repeated metaphor employed in much Puritan writing to characterize their mission is that of a single body. Bradford includes in his history a letter from John Robinson and William Brewster, two emissaries to the Virginia Company, in which is written, "We are knit together as a body in a most strict and sacred bond and covenant of the Lord . . . straitly tied to all care of each other's good and of the whole" (34). This image is in marked contrast to the actuality of the New England mission, however. Bradford, always a fastidious chronicler, included another correspondence in his history, one that presages the dissension that was to challenge Puritan religious authority in the future. In a letter to Edward Southworth, Robert Cushman, a member of the Leyden church since 1609 and leading organizer of the voyage to Plymouth, offered a more realistic view of this community: "Friend, if ever we make a plantation, God works a miracle, especially considering how scant we shall be of victuals, and most of all ununited amongst ourselves. . . . Violence will break all" (64). The juxtaposition of these missives reveals the divergent voices that would challenge the religious leadership of New England and set in motion a redefinition of prenational identity.[10]

The people of New England were a people in transition whose diverse religious beliefs and economic situations and whose constant contact with other races made group definition along secular rather than religious lines inevitable. Noticeable in the works of those Puritans bridging the older and younger generations of this community is an awareness of this inevitability. The work of one of New England's most prolific writers, Cotton Mather, affords an opportunity to note how, in this "middle passage" of New England writing, after migration and before revolution, issues of race, class, and gender are increasingly engaged to mark English-Puritan identity as white.

The grandson of John Cotton and the son of Increase Mather, Cotton Mather embodied three generations of Puritan thought and the social power exercised by a family of theologians. He produced copious sermons, treatises, jeremiads, and histories, all meant to sustain the Puritan vision. Three works in particular exemplify Mather's ability to create a discourse that preserved the spiritual past while constructing contemporary models for social relations: *Magnalia Christi Americana* (1702), *The Negro Christianized* (1706), and *A Good Master Well Served* (1696).

Mather's most substantial single volume, the *Magnalia*, is characterized by scholar Sacvan Bercovitch as an "immense work—packed with narratives, sermons, church decrees, and biographies . . . 'a mighty chaos,' flung together huge and undigested and groaning with ostentatious erudition and verbal bombast" (in Emerson, 137). Written in hindsight, it uses past as prologue and celebrates personages such as William Bradford and Massachusetts Bay Colony governor John Winthrop. It preserves selected moments of history and illuminates aspects of philosophy that Mather thought exemplary for New England.

Unlike Bradford's more immediate history, Mather's *Magnalia* is a deliberate retelling of already-written fact, a twice-told tale. Its embellishments and emphases suggest, therefore, what events, characteristics, and cultural values a religious and economic elite sought to enshrine as part of their written history and, by extension, the written historical record of their emerging nation. The *Magnalia* effects, for example, a conspicuous marginalization of groups that are not white. Though Mather spent much of his time organizing efforts to convert

Native Americans and to educate African American slaves, these groups are either excluded from his mytho-history of New England or, in the case of Native Americans, cast as hindering the region's progress. In the formal record Mather intends as a legacy, New Canaan is monocultural and monoracial, even if New England is not. As such, the *Magnalia* is one of the first documents to erase American diversity and write America as white.

In the *Magnalia*, Mather reiterated for a new generation the myth of Puritan pilgrims coming to the New World; but his flourishes began to racialize this enterprise, as is evident in his description of a plague that decimated much of New England's Native American population prior to English arrival:

> And yet behold the watchful Providence of God over them that seek him! . . . Had they been carried according to their desire unto *Hudson's River*, the *Indians* in those Parts were at this time so Many, and so Mighty, and so Sturdy, that in probability all this little feeble Number of Christians had been Massacred by these bloody Salvages, as not long after some others were: Whereas the good Hand of God now brought them to a Country wonderfully prepared for their Entertainment, by a sweeping *Mortality* that had lately been among the Natives. . . . The *Indians* in these Parts had newly, even about a Year or Two before, been visited with such a prodigious Pestilence; as carried away not a *Tenth*, but *Nine Parts* of *Ten*, (yea, 'tis said, *Nineteen of Twenty*) among them: So that the *Woods* were almost cleared of those pernicious Creatures, to make Room for a *better Growth*. (129)

What Bradford's history details impartially and sympathetically Mather's recasts as an act of unmerciful divine intervention.[11] A plague is not a plague but a means of preparing the New World for Puritan settlement. This passage is one instance of the conscious construction of a myth that has as one of its central themes, the contestation between two races, and as one of its central strategies, racial typing. Contrasting his people to Native Americans, Mather wrote, "This blessed People was as *a little Flock of Kids*, while there were many Nations of *Indians* left still as Kennels of *Wolves* in every Corner of the Country. And yet the *little Flock* suffered no damage by those Rabid *Wolves!*" (133). Mather's tone and language in this passage give race stereotypical content. Whites portrayed as meek lambs are juxtaposed to Native Americans represented as rapacious wolves, in a manner that would influence the racial perceptions of his readers (and subsequent generations of readers) and continues to define whiteness along a savage–civilized continuum.

This typing of Mather's Native American subjects as animalistic is paralleled by his typing of African Americans as uncivilized in his sermon *The Negro Christianized*. As much as it pleads for the conversion and baptism of slaves, *The Negro Christianized* shapes racial relations. It is ostensibly a religious imperative that prompts Mather's discourse, but embodied in his religious imperative is a racial hierarchy. Hand in glove with arguments for Christianizing Africans and their African American descendants go arguments asserting that social order is best maintained if they are baptized not only into a holy state but also into a social state in which they are subservient. Their catechisms should thus be "Suited to their poor Capacities" (28) and should be filled with what John Blassingame calls the "slave's beatitudes," those religious principles which teach that the service of earthly masters is equivalent to the service of God.[12] "Tell them," Mather exhorted his parishioners, "*That if they Serve God patiently and cheerfully in the Condition which he orders for them, their condition will very quickly be infinitely mended, in Eternal Happiness*" (32).

In his sermon, Mather created a series of contrasts that crystallized the image of a cultivated white civilization against an uncultivated black one. He compared the ancestors of Africans to the ancestors of the English: "'Tis true; They are *Barbarians*. But so were our own *ancestors*" (23). The gesture of equity in casting whites as the descendants of barbarians is undermined by the use of different tenses. Africans *are* barbarian; whites *were*. Mather's sermon makes references to African skin color and intellectual ability and implicitly highlights the superiority of white European attributes: that "Their *Complexion* sometimes is made an Argument, why nothing should be done for them" (24) reinforces the notion that the complexion most amenable to cultivation is white; that "their *Stupidity* is a *Discouragement*" (25) reinforces the notion of white intellectual superiority. The foregrounding of white identity against black again illustrates the recurring pattern of using nonwhiteness to give whiteness form.[13]

Racial contrasts were one means by which whiteness was composed. Another was the consistent association of whiteness with particular ideals and traits, such as freedom and social mobility. Early instances of this second strategy are evident in another Mather sermon, *A Good Master Well Served*. Sharing many similarities with *The Negro Christianized*—both stress the need for social stratification, both urge servants to obey masters, and both instruct in humane forms of discipline—*A Good Master* distinguishes itself from the former document in its assertion of the potential for white social elevation. Though much of the sermon's content demonstrates that in seventeenth-century New England the distinction between white servants and black servants or slaves was often more nominal than actual, it nonetheless links the promise of mobility and self-mastery to being white. In speaking of teaching servants, Mather admonished their employers, "You are also faithfully to TEACH your Servants the *Work* of that Calling. . . . While you use them for *Servants*, you must so use them, that in Time they may come to be *Masters*" (12). The uplift implied here is completely absent from *The Negro Christianized*, which stresses the permanence of black servitude. Mather explained to the owners of slaves, "The State of your *Negroes* in this World, must be low, and mean, and abject; a State of Servitude. No *Great Things* in this World, can be done for them. Something then, let there be done, towards their welfare in the *World to Come*" (*Negro Christianized*, 14). *A Good Master* amounts to a racial etiquette that distinguishes between servant and slave and racializes each. White skin bestows the privilege of self-betterment and the possibility of autonomy in the future.

The *Magnalia*, *The Negro Christianized*, and *A Good Master Well Served* offered all who could hear Mather preach, in addition to those beyond his area who could afford to purchase his published works, instruction in the appropriate divisions between races and classes.[14] These documents spanning the period of 1696–1706 reveal how conceptions of what is English, what is Puritan, and what is white were becoming increasingly blurred amid the presence of other races. Mather's imagining of an ideal Puritan community incorporates representations of race that would subsequently allow his writings to be read also as the imagining of an ideal white community. Amid his nostalgia for the Puritan past can be found the nascent constructions of whiteness that would ultimately lend coherence to a population of many European ethnicities, religions, and classes in constant contact with non-European peoples. It would be more popular documents, however, that would shape the qualities of whiteness sketched in Mather's pieces—civility, cultivation, piousness, social mobility—into early representations of actual racial types.

Captives and Criminals

In early travel narratives and visionary works, the outlining of white identity can be noted in how white peoples are contrasted to others in prenational America. Sketchy outlines are replaced with detailed portraits, however, in two extremely popular genres: the captivity narrative and the criminal narrative.

Of the captivity narratives, scholars Alden T. Vaughan and Edward W. Clark note the following:

> These stories were immensely popular because—like any successful literature—they served readers a hearty fare of lit-

erary and psychological satisfaction, peculiar to their time and place. In a society without fiction and plays, and almost barren of poetry, real-life dramas filled a crucial cultural void. . . . [T]ales of Indian captivity . . . told of raids and forced marches, of the wilderness and its native inhabitants, of the chilling efforts of Indians and Frenchmen to assimilate their captives into an alien culture.[15] (3)

Captivity narratives recount intimate encounters between cultures, races, and religions and employ consistent motifs to do so: meek English settlers are beset by savage Native Americans; pious Puritans resist the corruption of papist sects; helpless women and children surmount the vicissitudes of being prisoners in an alien culture.[16] Read over and over because of their drama and popularity, they cemented in readers' minds conceptions of "us" and "them." As Richard Slotkin observes, "Through repeated appearances and recastings in the literary marketplace, a narrative which proved viable as a bestseller . . . would be imitated. . . . Thus the experience would be reduced to an imitable formula, a literary convention. . . . When enough literature had been written employing the convention, it might become . . . a set of tacit assumptions on the nature of human experience, on human and divine motivations, on moral values, and on the nature of reality" (20). Racial perceptions are among the tacit assumptions Slotkin identifies. Continual references linking Native Americans and blackness, referring to Native American religion as devil worship, and depicting English suffering against the backdrop of Native American cruelty and barbarism created the many racial caricatures and themes that helped strengthen developing conceptions of whiteness.[17] The ultimate effect on the narratives' readers was the creation of group identity, solidified through feelings of identification, compassion, and fear. Readers were able to share the experiences of "heroes" and "heroines" who, despite losing self-mastery; being bartered as commodities, and eating the food, partaking in the economies, and often wearing the garb of their captors, were able to retain their cultural and, by extension, racial identities.[18]

The narratives can be read as cultural performance acts that dramatize characteristics representing first Puritan, then English, and subsequently white identity. They cement images of what whiteness is by creating images of what whiteness is not. For example, fervent and vivid language describing Native American barbarity helps reinforce conceptions of English white identity as civil. Published in 1682, Mary Rowlandson's narrative employs language that repeatedly casts Native Americans as rapacious predators while casting the English as hapless martyrs:

> Some in our house were fighting for their lives, others *wallowing in their blood*, the house on fire over our heads, and the *bloody heathen* ready to knock us on the head if we stirred out. . . . But out we must go, the fire increasing, and coming along behind us, roaring, and the Indians *gaping* before us with their guns, spears, and hatchets, to *devour* us. . . . When we are in prosperity, oh the little that we think of such dreadful sights, and to see our dear friends and relations ly *bleeding out their heart-blood*

upon the ground. . . . It is a solemn sight to see so many *Christians* lying in their blood, some here, and some there, like a *company of sheep torn by wolves*, all of them stript naked by a company of *hell-hounds*, roaring, singing, *ranting*, and *insulting*, as if they would have *torn our very hearts out.* (10–12; italics mine)

Rowlandson continued, "Oh the *roaring*, and singing, and dancing, and yelling of those *black* creatures *in the night*, which made the place a lively resemblance of hell" (13, italics mine). Her confederating blackness, the devil, hell, and Native Americans idealizes whiteness in negation to these elements. Rowlandson employed this strategy of contrast in another passage, portraying what she saw as the innate duplicity of Native Americans who adopted the Christian tradition. A series of descriptions continually pair the phrase "praying Indian" with relations of non-Christian acts and create an association that undermines the verity of Native American conversion:

There was another praying Indian who told me that he had a brother that would not eat horse, his conscience was so tender and scrupulous (though large as hell, for the destruction of poor Christians). . . . There was another praying Indian who, when he had done all the mischief that he could, betrayed his own father into the English hands, thereby to purchase his own life. . . . There was another praying Indian, so wicked and cruel as to wear a string about his neck, strung with Christian's fingers. (44)

In Rowlandson's prose, "praying Indian" seems an oxymoron. She essentially racialized salvation by intimating that even if baptized, savages would still be savages. The chosen ones are chosen not only by faith but also by race, and conversion is not sufficient to remove racial traits. Racial difference is immutable, unalterable even by religious transformation.

Race is not the only backdrop against which white identity is foregrounded, however. Scenes in many captivity narratives detail religious contestations that establish Protestantism as the religious ideal of whiteness. In his narrative of captivity, John Williams, a Congregational minister in Deerfield, Massachusetts, included lengthy passages critiquing Catholicism. In one he recalled:

> After a day or two the Jesuits asked me what I thought of their way now [that] I saw it? I told them I thought Christ said of it as Mark 7:7–9: "Howbeit in vain do they worship me, teaching for doctrines the commandments of man. For laying aside the commandment of God, ye hold the tradition of men as the washing of pots and cups and many such like things ye do. And He said unto them, 'Full well ye reject the commandment of God that ye may keep your own tradition.' " They told me they were not the commandments of men but apostolical traditions of equal authority with the holy Scriptures. And that after my death I would bewail my not praying to the Virgin Mary. . . . I told them it was my comfort that Christ was to be my judge and not they at the Great Day, and, as for their censuring and judging of me, I was not moved with it. (Vaughan and Clark, 185)

Similarly, John Gyles in his narrative wrote, "Mr. Woodbury asked me whether I designed to go [see a Jesuit banish blackbirds from a field of wheat]. I told him that I did. He said that I was then as bad a papist as they and a damned fool. I told him that I believed as little of it as they did, but I inclined to see the ceremony that I might rehearse it to the English" (Vaughan and Clark, 127). Just as racial notions were solidified through constant repetition, so were religious ones. By continually casting Catholicism as a misguided attempt at worship, Protestantism was privileged and the ruling clerical elite of New England were able to sustain their social power.

As well as shaping specific racial and religious ideologies, representations of white identity in the captivity narratives shaped conceptions of gender. As Vaughan and Clark note, a female captive was often depicted as "a passive mother who witnessed the murder of her baby and the abduction of her older children by a cruel man-monster. Although the actual experience of captive women often justified a more assertive image, the usual picture in the public mind was of a frail woman submissively kneeling before her Indian captor, waiting for a death stroke from a raised tomahawk" (25). The passivity Vaughan and Clark describe is visible in the narrative of Elizabeth Hanson (1728). As her children are killed, Hanson looks on helplessly:

[T]wo of my younger children, one six and the other four years old, came in sight and, being under a great surprise, cried aloud, upon which one of the Indians, running to them, takes one under each arm and brings them to us. My maid prevailed with the biggest to be quiet and still, but the other could by no means be prevailed with but continued screeching and crying very much in the fright, and the Indians, to ease themselves of the noise and to prevent the danger of a discovery that might arise from it, immediately before my face knocked its brains out. (Vaughan and Clark, 231–32)

Hanson's recollections are indicative of the narratives' increasing depiction of white women as ineffectual.[19] The repeated portrayals of white women as defenseless, dependent, incapable, and powerless defined white women as needing the protection of white men. Whiteness, then, effectively became a racial identity embodying gender values in which males were empowered and females disempowered. While representations of white women embodied race privilege, they did not embody gender equity. Challenges to this patriarchal tableau would be expressed in writings of the late eighteenth and nineteenth centuries through a variety of subversive literary techniques, among which is the repeated trope of white female identification with racially marginalized groups.[20]

As the narratives developed as a genre, the gender divide deepened, and representations of white women evolved from the lone, capable white female wielding a musket and fending off attackers who was depicted on the cover of the 1773 edition of Rowlandson's narrative (Figure 6) to women in need of male protection. In later reprints of captivity narratives, visual images of women are more in keeping with nineteenth-century conceptions of the "cult of true womanhood" than with Puritan conceptions of women as able helpmates.[21] For example, John Frost's 1846 *Pictorial History of the United States of America from the Discovery by the Northmen in the Tenth Century to the Present*

A
NARRATIVE
OF THE
CAPTIVITY, SUFFERINGS AND REMOVES
OF
Mrs. *Mary Rowlandfon*,

Who was taken Prifoner by the INDIANS with feveral others, and treated in the moft barbarous and cruel Manner by thofe vile Savages : With many other remarkable Events during her TRAVELS.

Written by her own Hand, for her private Ufe, and now made public at the earneft Defire of fome Friends, and for the Benefit of the afflicted.

BOSTON:

Printed and Sold at JOHN BOYLE's Printing-Office, next Door to the *Three Doves* in Marlborough-Street. 1773.

1773

---

6. This woodcut accompanying Mary Rowlandson's captivity narrative reflects a self-sufficiency subsequently lost in popular representations of white women. (COURTESY, AMERICAN ANTIQUARIAN SOCIETY)

Time uses prevalent nineteenth-century views of women. In one illustration, a dark-haired woman is on her knees, flanked by two Native American men. One waves a tomahawk menacingly, and the other, in what might be a gesture of protection, raises a forbidding hand to stop the delivery of the fatal blow. As much as it represents the helplessness of a white female, this image and others like it evoke potential sexual violation. They represent an increasing concern with white sexual purity and, by extension, white race purity.[22] Loss of sexual purity through intercourse with other races endangers visible race difference, a key driving force behind an ideology of whiteness that gives political, economic, and social advantages to those with the "appropriate" racial lineage. That the white woman is made the locus of this race purity illustrates the sexual license patriarchy grants white men by sanctioning white male sexuality and denying white female sexuality. This, along with portrayals of nonwhite sexuality as licentious, helps construct the myth of white sexual restraint. The imagined loss of sexual purity evoked by the state of captivity thus provided an opportunity for idealizing the inherent asexual nature of whiteness, and the captivity genre set the stage for differentiating white identity along lines not only of skin color, religion, and nationality but also of sexual morality. This last element in the pantheon of whiteness would be developed further in the more secularized genre of criminal narrative.

Captivity narratives were stories born out of contestations that had the claiming of land as their genesis. Once the land

was settled and communities were established, different contestations emerged and fostered the creation of another genre,
the criminal narrative. Widely interpreted as responses to social
upheaval, criminal narratives developed initially as a means of
maintaining social control in a contentious climate. During the
mid-seventeenth century and beyond, New England experienced radical change. King Philip's War and other conflicts
with Native American nations, and an increasing African and
African American presence, accentuated racial tensions. Puritan intolerance of other sects fanned religious dissension. The
printing of colonial currency and New England's violation of
the 1660 and 1663 Navigation Acts led to English suspension
of charters and to the lessening influence of the mother country
in colonial affairs. Finally, loss of crops, loss of goods to piracy
on the high seas, and loss of labor power due to epidemics
fostered a concern with material security that weakened the
spiritual notion of New England as a religious "city upon a
hill."[23] The criminal narratives became one means of mediating
these transmutations through the medium of literature.

According to scholar Daniel Cohen, by the 1730s, when the
narratives enjoyed great popularity,

> A social order still closely regulated by Puritan ministers and
> magistrates had gradually evolved into a more conflicted and
> cosmopolitan milieu. Opposition factions contested political
> authority; members of various religious denominations wor-
> shipped openly; clubs, coffeehouses, and taverns flourished;
> several local newspapers circulated freely . . . and aggressive

printers, publishers, and booksellers vied for the patronage of an expanded reading public. (17)

One way in which religious magistrates attempted to buttress their eroding power was by employing occasions of public execution as symbolic warnings. These events garnered a great deal of public attention, and various estimates list crowds into the thousands in attendance. The last moments of those condemned were recounted in jeremiads, sermons used to warn increasingly worldly flocks of the fates awaiting them should they not repent. As literary critic Daniel Williams notes,

> Public execution was an elaborately staged ritual drama. . . . During their confrontation with death, and because of their proximity to death, condemned criminals were . . . figures of power and influence . . . since death gave their words the conviction of profound truth. Those responsible for staging their deaths attempted to use the force of this truth to shape social behavior. . . . When presented in popular narratives, criminal characters functioned . . . to reinforce civil authority and social conformity. (*Pillars of Salt*, x)

Not only were the executions a means of reinforcing religious and social authority, but because they appeared in written documents disseminated to a broad audience, some of whom might read of executions without having attended them, they became venues for constructing social and racial identities.

Created for the masses, the executions reasserted lines of social power and further delineated notions of idealized whiteness. Condemned criminals represented the danger of breaking the social order, but more important, they personified the qualities condemned by that order. While these qualities were initially cast in the narratives as general human failings, gradually particular failings were attached to specific class, gender, ethnic, and racial groups. By the time criminal narratives were produced in the 1780s and 1790s, consistent patterns were evident: women "were characterized as succumbing to the weaknesses of their sex. . . . With one or two exceptions . . . all [criminals] were relatively young, and all lacked the privileges and power reserved for members of the elite. . . . Consistently, the narratives dramatized the lives of capital offenders who were either Irish or black" (Williams, *Pillars of Salt*, 51–52). The criminal narratives made acute those representations that in travel narratives, religious writings, and captivity narratives define whiteness more obliquely as "none of the above": not Native American, not African, not Catholic, and not of certain European ethnicities. They followed the tendency characterized by Richard Slotkin when he notes, "In societies that are still in the process of achieving a sense of identity, the establishment of a normative, characteristic image of the group's character is a psychological necessity; and the simplest means of defining or expressing the sense of such a norm is by rejecting some other group whose character is deemed to be the opposite" (68). Through what they represented as *not* desirable, criminal narratives explicated the traits that were deemed desirable for white identity: consistently emphasizing the lower-class status of criminals classified the ideal identity as one stemming from the upper classes; emphasis on the non-

European identity of the perpetrator reinforced the notion that that moral and normative identity was European; regularly demarking undesirable ethnicity further restricted the ideal to not just European origins but English origins; and repeatedly rendering female characters as weak clearly perpetuated gender difference within this identity.

In these narratives, as in the captivity narratives, whiteness is given form by contrast to another race. Where in the captivity narratives this contrast was accomplished primarily with images of Native Americans, in the criminal narratives images of African Americans predominate. In most cases the content of African American criminal narratives does not differ markedly from that of white narratives retelling acts of theft, rape, murder, or drunkenness; but the visuals accompanying these stories of transgressions do. In *Revolution and the Word* (1986), Cathy N. Davidson analyzes the impact of graphics on a narrative's appeal and in doing so provides a means of understanding how racial notions might be analogously manipulated: "A fairly innocuous sentence could easily be given a more sensational cast by the strategic italicizing or capitalizing of words such as SEDUCTION or INCEST. Such printing devices naturally helped to sell books" (20). Similarly, such devices helped cement racial ideas. Many criminal narratives explicitly linked race and rape in their frontispieces. The subtitle of *Sketches of the Life of Joseph Mountain* (1790) continues with the words "A NEGRO" capitalized, and "For a Rape" in a large font. Likewise, the subtitle of *The Narrative and Confession of Thomas Powers* (1796) capitalizes "A NEGRO" and "RAPE" (Figure 7).

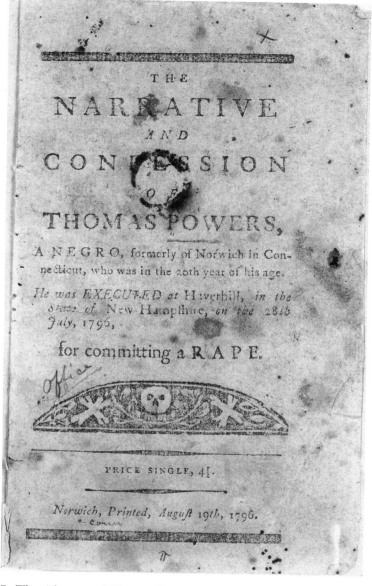

THE

NARRATIVE

AND

CONFESSION

OF

THOMAS POWERS,

A NEGRO, formerly of Norwich in Connecticut, who was in the 20th year of his age.

He was EXECUTED at Haverhill, in the
State of New Hampshire, on the 28th
July, 1796,

for committing a R A P E.

PRICE SINGLE, 4½.

Norwich, Printed, August 19th, 1796.

7. The title page of Thomas Powers's narrative titillates by reinforcing notions of race and sexual depravity. (LIBRARY OF CONGRESS
RARE BOOK READING ROOM)

Subliminal associations of race and sexual degeneracy were not limited to the frontispieces, however. In an addendum to Joseph Mountain's tale, one magistrate comments:

> The crime which you are convicted, is of a *deep dye*, is very heinous in the sight of God and man, and in most if not all the civilized nations, punishable with death: It was by you committed with every circumstance of aggravation . . . glorying in your shame, and even insulting the victim of your *brutal* lust . . . . [Y]ou, regardless of the all-piercing eye of . . . God . . . , wholly inattentive to human discovery, or the detection of your *dark designs*, meeting the harmless and innocent maid . . . urged on by worse than *brutal lust*, and more than *savage barbarity* . . . with force and violence ravished her of what to a female is as dear as life, and which leaves her, (tho' an object of pity and compassion) to spend the remainder of her days in grief and sorrow. (Williams, *Pillars of Salt*, 305, italics mine)

It is difficult to miss the double entendre of phrases such as "deep dye" and "dark designs" and how these resonate with racial overtones when used in castigating an African American male subject. These references, augmented by others such as "brutal lust" and "savage barbarity," "color" rape and reinforce notions of the sexually degenerate Other. In contrast, as Daniel Williams notes, "Readers were not presented with narratives of white masters raping servants or slaves" (in Shuffelton, 218); thus white identity, in implicit comparison to black, was rendered as noncarnal and morally superior. The content of frontispieces and addenda contributed to casting sexual reserve as a characteristic of whiteness. Employing images of depraved nonwhite sexuality securely located virtue in white identity and privileged it by rendering it morally superior.

Along with the disparagement of particular racial groups, the narratives also reveal instances where ethnic groups are systematically stereotyped. *The American Bloody Register*, one of the nation's earliest crime gazettes, included in its 1784 edition the narratives of three thieves, one of whom was also convicted of murder. In each, not only the crime but also the ethnicity of the criminal is emphasized. The three narratives begin in the same manner:

> I *RICHARD BARRICK*, was born in *Ireland*, in the month of February . . .

> I *JOHN SULLIVAN*, was born in *Ireland* in the town of *Limrick* . . .

> *This* is to give satisfaction to all enquiring Friends, that I *ALEXANDER WHITE*, was born in *Ireland*, in the County of *Tyrone* . . . (Williams, *Pillars of Salt*, 234, 238, 242)

That these narratives appear back to back in the first number of the register shows a repeated linkage of crime to Irishness. This pairing served to continue the hierarchizing of European ethnicities and again reveals that at this time, in its nascent state, whiteness was not yet a unified racial identity. Additionally, at a time when few Irish were part of the ruling elite of colonial America, this repeated parallel served to locate criminal behavior within not only a particular ethnic group but also within a particular caste group, the working or lower class. The insinuated class division here reveals the mutating nature of class within whiteness. The ideal of white identity incorporates economic privilege, yet when faced with the specter of a non-white race, it elides class difference in the interest of racial solidarity.

As the representations of race, class, and ethnicity contributed their respective privileges to the construction of an ideology of whiteness, so representations of gender in the criminal narratives contributed the privilege of masculinity. In much of this genre, women are shown to be easily corruptible when not under the influence of fathers, husbands, or male clerics. In Cotton Mather's compendium *Pillars of Salt* (1699), a collection that evolved from his execution sermons, he frequently portrayed women as adulteresses, weak-willed victims of their sexual desires, and he also related numerous instances of infanticide. One selection tells of a pregnant woman who is said to have "concealed her Crime, till the Time of her Delivery; and then, being Delivered alone, by her self in a Dark Room, She Murdered the harmless and helpless *Infant*; hiding it in a Chest, from the Eyes of all, but the Jealous GOD" (in Williams, *Pillars of Salt*, 66). In another, "Two Young Women, (the one *English*, t'other *Negro*) were Executed at *Boston*, for murdering their *Bastard Children*" (in Williams, *Pillars of Salt*, 86). As the rest of this narrative unfolds, only the story of the English-woman is given (again, the early reference here is to nationality, not race), and the black woman's experience, inconsequential to constructing lines of white gender, is erased. Another segment depicts the inability of Sarah Smith to exhibit moral continence. After being accused of adultery and stealing, she received religious counsel and "for a while . . . led a Reformed life. . . . But e're it was long, she lost her Seriousness, her Tenderness, her Convictions; and Relapsed into the Sin of *Adultery*. Her first Relapse into that Sin, was attended with a *Conception*, which, tho' she endeavored for to render it an Abortive, the Holy providence of God would not suffer it to be so. She did, with much Obstinacy, Deny and Conceal her being with *Child*: and when the *Child* was Born, she smothered it" (in Williams, *Pillars of Salt*, 88).

Independently published narratives impart similar portraits. The narrative of Patience Boston (1738) describes her mendacity in denying the killing of three children and then her subsequent killing of an eight-year-old in her charge. The narrative of Elizabeth Wilson (1786) depicts her standing by as the lover who spurned and abandoned her kills their infant twins. One narrative in particular demonstrates the voyeuristic nature of this genre. The introduction to the conversion narrative of Esther Rodgers (1701) opens with an image inviting readers to "view" the spectacle of a Rodgers's redemption before death: "Reader; *This Serves only to draw the Curtain, that thou mayst behold a Tragick Scene, strangely changed into a* Theater *of* Mercy, *a* Pillar of Salt *Transformed into a Monument of Free Grace*" (in Williams, *Pillars of Salt*, 95). The theater metaphor suggests the narratives' capacity to function as both cautionary tales and entertainment designed to reach a broad and popular audience.

The possible causes of female infidelity and of infanticide and the ways in which property rights and inheritance laws

marginalized women are buried deep beneath narratives showing female weakness and perversion.[24] Perhaps representations
constructed during the first third of the eighteenth century,
when gender restrictions were increasingly challenged, responded to the new roles women began to adopt for themselves, as described by historian Lyle Koehler:

> A leisure class of women had emerged, the wives of bewigged
> merchants and public officials. Unwilling to respect Puritan in-
> junctions against the evils of idleness, these women not only
> dressed well, but often amused themselves with card games. . . .
> Others, the young as well as the elderly, were either unwilling
> or unable to experience a leisurely lifestyle but, of necessity,
> worked in a self-supportive capacity. . . .
>
> The number of female innkeepers shot upward. . . .
>
> Educational opportunities for middle-class girls expanded
> during the 1690s, with at least three matrons and three men
> opening coeducational private schools in Boston. (430–31)

Changing definitions of women challenged prevailing patriarchal and religious authority in New England, and the narratives
might be read as backlashes against women's progress. They
continue the myth of Eve, the seductress whose moral fallibility
led to expulsion from Eden, and thus demonize women while
reinforcing male authority.

As they matured as a genre, the criminal narratives' content
increasingly delineated a desirable identity by propagating negative representations of other identities. Over the course of
their evolution, they became less concerned with conversion

and religious salvation and more concerned with titillations of sexual encounter, robbery, and the flouting of traditional institutions. They reflected their readers' desires and shaped their readers' perceptions. Their repetition of consistent racial, ethnic, sexual, and gender images and their dissemination of these images to a broad popular audience enabled them to propagate widely notions of what constituted ideal whiteness: a white physical appearance; European origins, preferably English; Protestantism; sexual restraint; and clearly defined gender roles.

•

Travel documents, visionary writings, and narratives of crime and captivity illuminate the degree to which the construction of whiteness depended on the written word. Written matter in early New England aggregated racial representations, giving whiteness a position of privilege. Readers who would define themselves as white were connected to one another through the print medium, and a common identity formed as selected traits fueled the imagining of a racial community.[25] In writing, universal human characteristics—hard work, piousness, civility, cognitive ability, physical beauty—were repeatedly associated with one racial group, and as the centuries progressed, these traits would be elaborated on and standardized in records transcending time and geography. During the seventeenth and eighteenth centuries, the printed word became a key tool of the hegemony formalizing whiteness, and it was joined by other tools with the advent of the nineteenth century. Images of whiteness would be enshrined in newspapers, novels, museums, stage productions, songs, and other material culture objects, and the nebulous representations of early literature would become clear, coherent, and commonplace.

3

Of Whales
and Whiteness

Who would have looked for philosophy in whales, or
for poetry in blubber?
—*John Bull* review of *Moby-Dick*

MY SON'S FIFTH-GRADE class once took a field trip to Dumbarton House in Washington, D.C., home of Joseph Nourse, the first Register of the United States Treasury. When questioned about the presence of an African American in a stained-glass portrait of George Washington's family, the docent informed the children that many prominent Americans at the time had slaves, including Nourse, who did not want to own slaves but did nonetheless. She went on to observe that Nourse was very good to his slaves. When my son pointed out that had he really been good to them he would have freed them, the docent replied that it was a different time back then.

The concept embodied in a phrase such as "It was a different time back then" is an interesting one, for it conveniently absolves past figures, particularly white American males, from ethical reproach. This notion is employed frequently, for example, as a rationale for American revolutionary figures who fought for their own liberty while simultaneously enslaving others. It is a notion that casts past figures as victims of supposedly monolithic attitudes of their time, and it ignores contestations to social inequity discoverable in every epoch of American history. In considerations of race, this rationale implies that awareness of racial injustice is a contemporary creation and gives no credit to thoughtful white men of the past who questioned the privilege afforded them because of their race and gender. An example of one such man of the nineteenth century is Herman Melville, who in a significant portion of his writing deconstructed a cultural ideology based on assumptions of white supremacy and questioned the impact of this ideology on an increasingly pluralistic nation.

By the time Melville was writing, the nebulous representations of whiteness as something vaguely English or vaguely Christian that are found in seventeenth- and eighteenth-century sermons, histories, travel, crime, and captivity narratives were giving way to fully fleshed literary characterizations in nineteenth-century fiction. Yankees, frontiersmen, Southern cavaliers, greenhorns, sexless and morally pure white women— all became standard models of white identity.[1] A novel such as James Fenimore Cooper's *The Last of the Mohicans* provides the opportunity to view more than one of these representations at work. In Cooper's fable readers are introduced to Hawkeye, a woodsman who describes himself as "genuine white" (31) yet is familiar with Native American language and culture and possesses a Native American's knowledge of the North American landscape. The literary descendant of real-life figures such as Daniel Boone, he epitomizes an indigenous American spirit not imitative of English traditions or bound to an established, eastern United States sensibility. An everyman hero, he represents white conquest of the American frontier.

Along with Hawkeye, readers meet Alice Munro, a racially pure white female with "fair golden hair" and "bright blue eyes" (18), who exhibits the feminine innocence and ineffectualness appropriate to Victorian ideals of femininity.[2] With assistance from Hawkeye, she is eventually united with the man who will be her betrothed, a young, noble, racially pure white male "born at the south" among "unfortunate beings . . . considered of a race inferior" to his (159): Major Duncan Heywood. Alice's sister, Cora, who in the middle of the novel we discover is actually her half sister, is intelligent, brave, beautiful, with "tresses . . . shining and black, like the plumage of the raven" and a "complexion . . . not brown, but . . . rather . . . charged with the colour of the rich blood, that seemed ready to bursts its bounds" (19). Her appearance betokens her misfortune of having African antecedents, and her end might be said to manifest Cooper's view that miscegenation can end only in tragedy. Other popular white representations are present in this novel in the form of French trappers, traders, and soldiers whose occasional lapses in scruples highlight the inherent honesty of English, Yankee, Protestant character; the chivalric military leader Colonel Munro, who signifies the Old World honor that is the foundation of American ideals; and David, a psalmodist whose religious ditties conjure up images of early

American religious orthodoxies now useless in a new frontier. Noteworthy is that at novel's close, any character that might complicate the vision of a pure white race settling and peopling the North American continent is removed. Cooper's "good" Indians have routed the "bad" ones, in the process have handily died out themselves or become insignificant, and, as the novel's final speech proclaims, "The pale-faces are masters of the earth" (350).

Cooper's personifications of whiteness simplify in literature a more complex body of ideas reflecting the needs and aspirations of many defining themselves as white Americans. His characters have aggregately conquered North America and established the supremacy of whites on its soil. Their actions appealed to elements of a nineteenth-century cultural imagination impassioned by new waves of nationalism and expansionism, as the popular reception of his novels suggests. There were, of course, all manner of contestations to the ideology represented by Cooper's characters. Continued slavery, continued Native American removals, the Mexican-American War, and the exploitation of Chinese Americans laboring on a transcontinental railroad produced alternative discourses that offered cultural representations of whiteness far different from Cooper's.[3]

Among the discourses was a massive, moody, and memorable novel. In it a multiracial, multicultural crew set sail on a craft named after an exterminated Native American people in search of a white leviathan. To borrow a phrase of from its author, "What could be more full of meaning?" (Melville, 40).

While novelists such as Cooper employed literary figures and themes that came to idealize whiteness, Melville offered a singular critique of the ideology giving meaning to these representations. The work's many allusions to literature, art, history, philosophy, theology, and pseudoscience mount a critique of how, over time, all these disciplines contributed to a complex system of values exalting whiteness as a racial and cultural ideal. Its engagement of a variety of cultural visions questions the privileging of a western European vision that subordinated others to its own. Under the guise of retelling a whaling voyage, Melville explores how symbols, myth, and common beliefs were enlisted to support the primacy of whiteness.

Though written in 1851, *Moby-Dick* may be said to have origins in the American Revolution, for many of its themes were generated by the contradictions this period laid bare. Without the specter of English domination to crystallize what it meant to be American, attempts to characterize the Republic's identity in formal and popular discourses turned inward and faced the challenge of making a national self out of a hybrid people from different racial, ethnic, religious, and class backgrounds. As discussed in Chapter 1, two key results of this introspection were that the social label of whiteness mitigated potential class strife among white ethnics and that more and more, whiteness became synonymous with Americanness as the identity of the nation was cemented to the identity of a single created race. The question of who was a "real" American was increasingly answered with the response that it was one who was white, thus giving this race a position of national privilege.

The inherent fallacy of this exclusionary definition is engaged in *Moby-Dick*. The novel reflects an acute awareness of racial and cultural pluralism while it dissects the cultural customs, disciplines, and values that create an ideology ignoring difference and privileging whiteness.

·

As a novel, *Moby-Dick* has undergone a variety of examinations, some considering its theological vision, others its literary influences, others its engagement of various philosophies.[4] If, as Leslie Fiedler notes, "The best criticism can hope to do is to set the work in as many illuminating contexts as possible" (10), then *Moby-Dick* has been the beneficiary of innumerable efforts. A relatively new "illuminating context" attempts to shed light on the racial vision within the novel. As literary critic Carolyn Karcher notes:

> Until the mid-1960s, there was almost no interest in Melville's racial views, and very little recognition of the prominent place that social criticism occupies in his writings. . . . Only since the Civil Rights and anti–Vietnam War movements have forced us to read our national history and literature afresh has it become possible to approach Melville with a different set of questions and assumptions about him as an artist, thinker, and moralist. (ix–x)

Karcher rightly observes that Melville has much to tell our nation about its attitude toward race, but studies examining this dimension of his writing focus chiefly on his treatment of the characters of color peopling his works and less on his analysis of the presumed superiority of whiteness.

In discussing Melville's racial vision, many scholars debate whether his sentiments are really as racially democratic as they seem and raise concerns similar to those voiced by Edward Stone:

> A democrat both in lower and upper case, a lover of mankind of whatever color,—Herman Melville was all of these, and a racist as well. In that inconsistency more than in any other way does he come into view in the telescope of time as the thinking, feeling citizen of his day. (349)

I suggest that the inconsistency Stone documents through Melville's portraits of nonwhite races reflects the complexities faced by a white racial identity acutely aware of its existence in a multiracial nation, a white racial identity in sympathy with the ideals of the American democratic project yet keenly aware of the undemocratic nature of its race relations. *Moby-Dick*'s portraits of nonwhites are only part of this awareness, however; the novel's other significant component is an exploration of what whiteness means in a culture of many races. As well as embodying a host of symbolic associations from purity to terror, Melville's white whale also embodies in a more concrete sense an audacious examination of the ways in which many cultural discourses—art, science, and history among them— conspire to create one racial group's privilege at the expense of others.

In the introduction to his edited anthology *Native American*

Testimony (1991), Peter Nabokov mentions the following Native American prophecy foretelling the arrival of Europeans: "On what is today Martha's Vineyard, an Indian seer said a great white whale would foretell the coming of a strange white race who would crowd out the red men" (5). While knowledge of this soothsaying cannot be attributed to Melville, the symbolism equating the white whale with the coming of Europeans provides a useful approach to Melville's own white leviathan, for it is through Moby Dick[5] that Melville explores the power of whiteness in the collective American imagination. While creating a work ostensibly narrating the hunting of a white whale, he offers as well an analysis of the ways in which whiteness, through a created ideology of racial and cultural supremacy, is given political, social, and economic privilege. For a white male writer in 1851 to pen such a volume was a remarkably visionary undertaking, bordering on the insurgent, as Toni Morrison notes in "Unspeakable Things Unspoken":

> But to question the very notion of white progress, the very idea of racial superiority, of whiteness as privileged place in the evolutionary ladder of humankind, and to meditate on the fraudulent, self-destroying philosophy of that superiority, to "pluck it out from under the robes of Senators and Judges," to drag the "judge himself to the bar,"—that was dangerous, solitary, radical work. Especially then. Especially now. (18)

Through his whale, Melville explores the symbolisms associated with whiteness, from the general to the racially specific. To comprehend Melville's endeavor, however, one must look not directly to the whale but around it. Moby Dick and his color are not in and of themselves significant; rather, they are free-floating signifiers to which different interpretations are attached, depending on perspective. Together they are a subterfuge, designed to undermine a garrison of presumed white superiority in an age whose nationalism and westward expansion might censure such an effort.

Moby-Dick is, at the very least, two novels: one detailing the *Pequod*'s quest for Moby Dick, and another whose passages on philosophy, history, art, and cetology probe the many justifications of white dominance manifest in western European and American thought.[6] At times the whale is a whale: yet at other times it is a vehicle for investigating the nature and formation of racial perceptions. Only the leviathan is a symbol large enough for the scope of Melville's undertaking, as he readily concedes in his characteristically tongue-in-cheek manner, through the voice of Ishmael:

> One often hears of writers that rise and swell with their subject, though it may seem but an ordinary one. How, then, with me, writing of this Leviathan? Unconsciously my chirography expands into placard capitals. Give me a condor's quill! Give me Vesuvius' crater for an inkstand! Friends, hold my arms! For in the mere act of penning my thoughts of this Leviathan, they weary me, and make me faint with their outreaching comprehensiveness of sweep. (456)

As I will show later, contemplation of the whale is so closely tied to contemplation of racial whiteness that Ishmael's observations here can be read as characterizing the daunting task of de-universalizing whiteness in a culture that automatically presumes its universal significance and desirability. In "The Whiteness of the Whale,"[7] a chapter some have characterized as enigmatic, Melville commences his deconstruction of the many myths of whiteness.

"The Whiteness of the Whale" begins with references to several symbolic evocations and connotations of whiteness, from the pure to the fearsome, from the impressionistic to the concrete, from the color to the race. As the chapter continues, commentary describing the beauty, regality, purity, and holiness of whiteness devolves into commentary describing those aspects that prompt Ishmael to note, "yet for all these accumulated associations, with whatever is sweet, and honorable, and sublime, there yet lurks an elusive something in the innermost idea of this hue, which strikes more of panic to the soul than that redness which affrights in blood" (189). Elsewhere Ishmael observes, "It was the whiteness of the whale that above all things appalled me" (188), and his subsequent ruminations focus on the "dark" side of whiteness. He mentions "the white bear of the poles, and the white shark of the tropics," and he questions, "what but their smooth, flaky whiteness makes them the transcendent horrors they are?" (189); he contemplates the albino in the following manner: "What is it that in the Albino man so peculiarly repels and often shocks the eye, as that sometimes he is loathed by his own kith and kin? . . . The Albino is as well made as other men—has no substantive deformity—and yet this mere aspect of all-pervading whiteness makes him more strangely hideous than the ugliest abortion" (191). He notes that all ghosts rise in a "milk-white fog . . . that even the king of terrors, when personified by the evangelist, rides on his pallid horse" (192). He concludes by marveling that whiteness is "at once the most meaning symbol of spiritual things, nay, the very veil of the Christian's Deity; and yet should be as it is, the intensifying agent in things the most appalling to mankind" (195).[8] What the varying and sometimes contradictory images of whiteness indicate, here and throughout the novel, is that interpretations of the significance of whiteness, whether mythic, theological, or material, are influenced by presumptions and contexts. The crazed Ahab, who seeks to impose significance on the whiteness of Moby Dick, is akin to a civilization that for its own ends seeks to impose a variety of significances on racial whiteness. As suggested by literary scholar Marsha Vick, whiteness has no single meaning:

> In "The Whiteness of the Whale," the narrator defamiliarizes the trope of whiteness as an essence by describing it as "the visible absence of color." . . . He tries to break down the stereotypes associated with whiteness by enumerating its symbolic meanings in American and other cultures, thereby taking away any single meaning of good or evil. . . . With the oxymoronic phrase "dumb blankness" . . . he dismisses whiteness as a symbol of superiority. (337)

Vick rightly notes that whiteness, "the visible absence of color," is given meaning through cultural contexts, and by offering a variety of interpretations, Melville negates the absolute correctness of any one. "The Whiteness of the Whale" reflects on the mutating significance of whiteness, and its perceived superiority is thus shown to be not intrinsic but rather the result of cultural construction.

Probing the significance of whiteness necessitates probing how racial meaning and content are fabricated in a culture, and as early as the novel's first symbolic gesture, that of a frail keeper of a schoolhouse dusting books, Melville's preoccupation with how cultural and ultimately racial meaning is created and passed on becomes evident:

> [The pale Usher—threadbare in coat, heart, body, and brain ... was ever dusting his old lexicons and grammars, with a queer handkerchief, mockingly embellished with all the gay flags of all the known nations of the world.] (xv)

The usher's relatively small gesture forges a link between meaning and its vessels. He works in an institution meant to pass on knowledge; the books he dusts are lexicons and grammars, volumes that gather words, codify meaning, structure expression, and standardize all these to a particular cultural norm. That he dusts these works with a handkerchief decorated with flags of the world calls to mind the cultural relativity that is part of all knowledge. Schools, grammars, and lexicons may supply accrued information, but the significance of that information varies with context.

The centrality of context to understanding is developed further in the novel's "Etymology" and "Extracts" sections, which follow the introduction of the usher. "Etymology" contains the lexical history of the term *whale* and instances of its occurrence in languages as varied as Hebrew, Latin, and Erronangoan. "Extracts" consists of "random allusions to whales" culled from "any book whatsoever, sacred or profane" (xvii). Taken together, "Etymology" and "Extracts" offer what seems an infinite number of perspectives from which to view the whale. They also offer an opportunity to note the many sources from which conceptions, whether of a whale or a race, are garnered. In "Extracts," however, Melville posits a caution: "you must not, in every case at least, take the higgledy-piggledy whale statements, however authentic, in these extracts, for veritable gospel cetology" (xvii). This statement, considered in light of the extensive number of extracts varying from the authoritative to the colloquial, warns that the credibility of all knowledge is subject to the fallibility of the source.

By the end of "Extracts" it becomes clear that when Melville suggests no knowledge can be completely trusted, much more than knowledge of a whale is viewed skeptically; also viewed with jaundiced eye is knowledge that hiearchizes the value of human beings. The sources he alludes to in "Extracts" range from the formal to the folk, but all are products that in one way or another have disseminated values and notions deriving from western European thought and have been employed at various points in the course of western European history to lionize that civilization over others: religious writings (the Bible—Job, Jonah, Psalms, Isaiah); historical and legal writings (John Stow, Edmund Burke, William Blackstone); travel narratives (William Cornelius Schouten, Thomas Edge, James

Cook); political discourses (Thomas Jefferson, Rabelais, Daniel Webster); literature (Shakespeare, John Milton, John Dryden, James Fenimore Cooper, Nathaniel Hawthorne, Alexander Pope); philosophy (Thomas Hobbes, Lucian, Plutarch); scientific discourses (J. Ross Browne, Georges Cuvier, Thomas Beale), and popular works, (the *New England Primer*, a whale song, a Nantucket song).[9] These and many other sources within this body of thought contribute to an ideology asserting the superiority of whiteness. While "Extracts" provides an idea of their number and variety, it is the more detailed cetology passages of the novel that provide real insight into how such sources construct cultural and racial meaning.

To the chagrin of some readers, much *of Moby-Dick* consists of seemingly endless passages devoted to cetology, but this science clearly serves symbolic ends within the text. Through this system of classification, Melville scrutinizes not only the whale but also systems that categorize human beings. Throughout the novel's cetological "digressions" are constant references linking whales and humans, and through these links, explorations seemingly about whales are transformed into explorations of the means by which a variety of cultural discourses have served to privilege whiteness, among them scientific inquiry, art, and religion. Contextualizing this examination is a chapter that questions the motives behind acts of classification.

The first twenty-three chapters of *Moby-Dick* are narrative ones that set the novel's action in motion. Chapter 24, "The Advocate," however, is one in which Ishmael introduces the reasons why an elaborate description of the whale and whaling is a meritorious enterprise and why one has not been ventured before. He begins by identifying "straw-dogs" that he will fell while making his argument for the importance of cetological investigation. Embedded in the statements he subsequently debunks are overtones similar to those employed in rhetorical strategies asserting the inferiority of non–western European civilizations when compared to their western European counterparts. Ishmael's catalog of antiwhale sentiment includes the following:

> The whale has no famous author, and whaling no famous chronicler . . .

> [W]halemen themselves are poor devils; they have no good blood in their veins.

> The whale himself has never figured in any grand imposing way. (111)

Although concerned with whales, each of these statements resonates with values often used to affirm the preeminence of white civilizations over others: the esteeming of written traditions, the designation of selected ancestries as notable, and participation in the march of western European civilization. Ishmael's subsequent dismissal of these presumptions with regard to whales simultaneously rebukes their arbitrariness when used to undergird perceptions of white superiority—by valuing written over oral expression, one pedigree over another, one history over another. His reproach is made applicable to theories about humans through the many parallels constructed between these two groups of mammals.

Present in Ishmael's cetology is the recurrent observation that we cannot judge the whale at face value. Because Melville at many points closely links notions of whales to notions of humankind, these chapters implicitly critique systems that take humans at face value and rank one group and their creations above another. In his attempt to categorize whales, for example, Ishmael notes, "First: The uncertain, unsettled condition of this science of Cetology is in the very vestibule attested by the fact, that in some quarters it still remains a moot point whether a whale be a fish" (136). After this comment, he launches into a sizable discussion of Carolus Linnaeus's study of species and this naturalist's not classifying a whale as a fish.

It is significant that Linnaeus is the subject of Ishmael's digression, for it was his distinction among species and varieties that fueled debates, in both the eighteenth and nineteenth centuries, over whether certain nonwhite races, particularly Africans and Native Americans, were of the same species as Europeans. The ultimate aim of those who used Linnaeus's nonhierarchical system of arranging humankind into four groups of the same species (*Homo Europaeus*, *Homo Asiaticus*, *Homo Afer*, and *Homo Americanus*) was to create a divide that justified the supremacy of the white race over others. His theories were applied to give a scientific veneer to the very unscientific study of racial difference, to mask anecdotal claims as verifiable science.[10] Melville's allusion to Linnaeus evokes the classification of both the natural world and of human beings and is one example of Melville's extending the reach of *Moby-*

Dick's cetology, enabling it to comment as much on humans as on whales.

In a similar passage, Ishmael contemplates what makes a whale a whale, and what differentiates the whale from others of its species and kind:

> [Y]et it is in vain to attempt a clear classification of the Leviathan, founded upon either his baleen, or hump, or fin, or teeth; notwithstanding that those marked parts or features very obviously seem better adapted to afford the basis for a regular system of Cetology than any other detached bodily distinctions, which the whale, in his kinds, presents. . . .
>
> But it may possibly be conceived that, in the internal parts of the whale, in his anatomy—there, at least, we shall be able to hit the right classification. Nay; what thing, for example, is there in the Greenland whale's anatomy more striking than his baleen? Yet we have seen that by his baleen it is impossible correctly to classify the Greenland whale. (140)

Here again is the echo of queries in other writings that sought the origins of physical difference in humankind. One such thinker who contemplated this difference, cited in the novel's opening "Extracts," was Thomas Jefferson. In *Notes on the State of Virginia* (1784), Jefferson mused over the origin of African American appearance: "Whether the black of the negro resides in the reticular membrane between the skin and scarf-skin, or in the scarf-skin itself; whether it proceeds from the colour of the blood, the colour of the bile, or from that of some other secretion, the difference is fixed in nature, and is as real as if its seat and cause were better known to us" (186). That the tone of Ishmael's discourse on the whale is so similar to other discourses on racial difference, Jefferson's being one example, again makes the cetology passages more than dissections of the whale; they become critiques of systems that go only skin deep in their classification of human worth. Ishmael's willingness to concede the uncertainty of using external evidence to reach complex conclusions regarding human essence is in marked contrast to thinkers so willing to call specious speculation fact. His acknowledging, "it is in vain to attempt a clear classification of the Leviathan, founded upon either his baleen . . . hump . . . fin, or teeth," questions the significance of differences "fixed in nature" and assessments of worth based upon them.

In Ishmael's continued examination of the whale, other theories often used to substantiate arguments of racial superiority are engaged, two of which are phrenology and its offshoot craniology. According to historian John Davies:

> Phrenology originated as an experimental science. . . . [I]ts true foundation was the theory that anatomical and physiological characteristics have a direct influence upon mental behavior. . . .
>
> The second cardinal belief of the new psychology was that the mind . . . is composed of independent and ascertainable faculties, some thirty-seven in number . . . elaborately catalogued under such rubrics as . . . Combativeness, Veneration, Benevolence, Adhesiveness, Amativeness, and Language. Third, the phrenologists believed that these aptitudes or propensities are localized in different "organs" or regions of the brain.

The final theorem was the most famous as well as the most controversial . . . . it was thought that a man could make a fairly accurate character analysis by studying the shape of a subject's head in conjunction with his temperament. (3–4)

Davies also describes the methods of disseminating phrenology's precepts in nineteenth-century America:

The manifold deductions from phrenological principles were taken up by a variety of reformers to rationalize their crusades. Thus a large volume of literature was produced upon many topics, and through lecturers, societies, magazines, books, and periodical articles phrenological tenets were dinned into American ears until the appropriation of their peculiar vocabulary by fiction and popular speech made them familiar to everyone. (xi)

With such widespread application, phrenology came to be adopted by those desirous of making racial claims to superiority. It was used to argue that it would take time and education for African Americans to become the intellectual equals of whites; it was used to prove that Native Americans were inherently savage.[11] By the time Melville composed *Moby-Dick*, phrenology had been widely adapted for popular consumption. O. S. Fowler, a self-styled authority on phrenology, along with his brother set up an office on 135 Nassau Street in New York City that evolved into a combination lecture-booking office, publishing house, and museum, where the public could pay for phrenological readings. The locale held a collection of cranial reproductions of famous personages, of animals, and of various exotic "savages." Phrenology also influenced the interpretation of literature and art, as various phrenological journals published studies of portrait paintings and fictional characters.

Of Melville's interest in phrenology Tyrus Hillway notes, "It is probably safe to assume that this interest arose out of his deeper concern with human character and conduct, as well as out of his natural appetite for knowledge of all types. The significant thing is that he was not, like others of his time, deceived by the pretensions of these two pseudo-sciences to respectability, but instead recognized the limitations of their methods and theories" (150). Through references to phrenology, Melville again rebukes systems of classification flawed by cultural prejudice. In what is perhaps the novel's most memorable phrenological passage, in which Ishmael compares Queequeg to George Washington, an equality of race is achieved through a subversion of pseudoscientific tenets. Of Queequeg Ishmael notes, "[H]is head was phrenologically an excellent one. It may seem ridiculous, but it reminded me of General Washington's head, as seen in the popular busts of him. It had the same long regularly graded retreating slope from above the brows, which were likewise very projecting, like two long promontories thickly wooded on top. Queequeg was George Washington cannibalistically developed" (50). Of this description Carolyn Karcher observes, "We need only recall that nineteenth-century Americans placed Washington side by side with Shakespeare at the pinnacle of human evolution—and consigned the African cannibal to its nadir—to measure the distance Ishmael has traveled" (70). The validity of Karcher's assessment can be found in many sources of the period, one example being Josiah

C. Nott and George R. Gliddon's *Types of Mankind* (1854). This work claims to be a compendium of "Ethnological Researches" and includes many a chart ranking, from high to low, the appearances and skulls of, among others, "Apollo," a "Negro," and a "Young Chimpanzee" (458–59). That Ishmael's insights counter this and other prevailing standards is evident in his description not only of Queequeg but also of futile attempts to read the whale's character from its brow. Inlaid in his observations is a profound critique of biological difference employed to substantiate racial superiority.

Ishmael's characterization of the whale's skull forges yet another connection between the whale and humans:

> If you unload his skull of its spermy heaps . . . you will be struck by its resemblance to the human skull. . . . Indeed, place this reversed skull (scaled down to the human magnitude) among a plate of men's skulls, and you would involuntarily confound it with them; and remarking the depressions on one part of its summit, in phrenological phrase you would say—This man had no self-esteem, and no veneration. (349)

This link is developed further into a reproach of the pseudo-science when Ishmael voices an assessment of where the true value of human worth should be found, not in surface appearances but in deeper qualities:

> Now, I consider that the phrenologists have omitted an important thing in not pushing their investigations from the cerebellum through the spinal canal. For I believe that much of a man's character will be found betokened in his backbone. (349)

Through the vehicle of cetological examination, Melville derisively treats "sciences" that attempt classification based on the readily observable and suggests these should be replaced by systems that examine more inherent criteria—the morality, principles, and ethics that constitute "backbone"—which are in varying degrees of evidence in every human, regardless of race. In so doing, he shakes the foundation of "scientific" justification that alleges white skin to be an incontestable indicator of superiority. Exposing the flaws of craniology and phrenology in the classification of whales points to the inadequacy of these systems in constructing hierarchies in which whiteness is the epitome of racial worth. *Moby-Dick*'s cetology ultimately casts as bogus pseudoscientific assessments of biological difference and the assertions of racial superiority that derive from them. The novel's critical eye is not reserved solely for science and pseudoscience, however; it views artistic creations as well, and how these, too, have perpetuated myths of racial superiority and inferiority.

In a fascinating analysis of Melville's allusions to art, art scholar Stuart Frank names chapters 55–57 of *Moby-Dick* the "pictorial" chapters and observes, "The order of the three 'pictorial' chapters is by no means arbitrary. They are arranged as a progression, from error towards truth, from inherited traditions to first hand experience, from superstition to revelation" (xvii).[12] These chapters are titled, respectively, "Of the Monstrous Pictures of Whales," in which is discussed antiquity's "pictorial delusions . . . found among the oldest Hindoo, Egyptian, and Grecian sculptures"; "Of the Less Erroneous

Pictures of Whales, and the True Pictures of Whaling Scenes," which treats portraits of whales in scientific annals and in the art of painters capable of "seizing the picturesqueness of things"; and "Of Whales in Paint; in Teeth; in Wood; in Sheet-Iron; in Stone; in Mountains; in Stars," which mounts a material-culture analysis of whale objects, such as "brass whales hung by the tail for knockers to the road-side door" (260, 267, 270), and of how the sensitized eye can imagine whales in mountains and stars. Frank characterizes these chapters' content thus:

> The erroneous, "monstrous" pictures are of whales in ancient superstition, the sea-monster and dragon-whale fantasies of the Old Masters, Old Testament illustrators, and adherents of pagan myth. . . .
>
> The "less erroneous" pictures of whales are merely that. . . . They are a middle ground, the sincere but flawed attempts of artists and scientists to organize a world they have not experienced at close range. . . .
>
> The third chapter stands out from the rest. . . . The title of this third chapter mentions nothing about *images* of whales, but refers to the whales themselves, as if to acknowledge the palpable continuity between these whalemen's whales and the Leviathan of Nature. (xvii–xix)

As Frank observes, Melville's chapter titles reflect a progression of understanding: from images crafted in ignorance and fear, reflecting the bogeys of the creator's mind, to renderings that blend realism and artistic imagination, to those that are commonplace and imply an intimate knowledge. This progression can be viewed as an illustration of the power of art, whether in the case of whales or humans, to canonize erroneous, imaginative, or speculative representations as well as to document changes in understanding. We have only to consider portrayals of Native Americans and African Americans in art to find examples of the link between racial perceptions and artistic renderings that Melville evokes in his pictorial chapters. The evolution of the Native American subject over the course of westward removals as embodied in paintings such as John Vanderlyn's menacing *The Death of Jane McCrea* (1804), George Catlin's verisimilar *Buffalo Hunt* (1844), and Thomas Moran's nostalgic *The Spirit of the Indian* (1869), for instance, reflects the progression from fear to anthropological understanding to an industrial-era nostalgia for a people symbolizing a now-vanished frontier. Similarly, the contrast between Eastman Johnson's nostalgic *Old Kentucky Home (Negro Life at the South)* (1859) and a *Harper's Weekly* cartoon, "Cutting His Old Associates" (1863), in which a former slave bids goodbye to chattel as if they were his equals and colleagues, reveals an evolving depiction of African Americans from docile to grotesquely laughable that reflects growing white anxiety over the social enfranchisement of a formerly enslaved people.[13] The allusions to art reveal the breadth of Melville's scrutiny of systems that reinforced an ideology of racial primacy. He deconstructs not only the obvious assertions of supremacy found in science and pseudoscience but also the more subtle visual representations of art and material culture, which have an even greater reach within a culture and thereby have an even greater power to cement racial notions throughout a culture.

Melville's inquiry in *Moby-Dick* is indeed a broad one, calling into question the many avenues of received knowledge that traditionally have been employed to subordinate races of color to whiteness. But while the novel critiques a supremacist ideology in which classification and hierarchy predominate, it also offers an antidote, an alternative vision of multicultural and multiracial equity. Through "a crew . . . chiefly made up of mongrel renegades, and castaways, and cannibals" (186), and through the motif of migratory quest, the novel revisits the theme of American encounter and rewrites it, creating a paragon in which the idea of democracy has not been consumed by the ideology of whiteness.

In the narrative of Ishmael's voyage Melville embeds many descriptions that recapitulate a white identity encountering its Other. Ishmael, a cipher, a lost child, a former teacher, is the perfect choice of narrator for this alternative history, for he is, as Edward Grejda describes him, "a meditative man, a Melville, given to probing the problem of the universe and the interrelationships of its creatures" (83). His progress through the novel leads him into continual contacts with races and cultures outside his own. Whatever surprise and consternation he experiences during these encounters, he generally adopts an attitude of cultural relativity that eventually leads to a spirit of cultural tolerance. Perhaps Melville's most illuminating example of Ishmael's process of cultural acceptance is the relationship that develops between him and Queequeg. When confronted with the unknown in his initial viewing of Queequeg, Ishmael's desire to discover and to know supersedes his fear of what to him is alien. He observes:

> I am no coward, but what to make of this head-peddling purple rascal altogether passed my comprehension. Ignorance is the parent of fear, and being completely nonplussed and confounded about the stranger, I confess I was now as much afraid of him as if it was the devil himself who had thus broken into my room at the dead of night. . . .
>
> But there was no time for shuddering, for now the savage went about something that completely fascinated my attention, and convinced me that he must indeed be a heathen. (21–22)

Though at first fearful of Queequeg, and though he initially dismisses him as a heathen, Ishmael's responses evolve, reflecting first curiosity and then an irresistible desire to understand Queequeg and his practices. Ultimately he concludes, "What's all this fuss I have been making about, thought I to myself— the man's a human being just as I am: he has just as much reason to fear me, as I have to be afraid of him" (24). The scene between the two as they awake in bed the next morning further symbolizes tolerance and connectedness as models for accommodating racial and cultural difference: "Upon waking next morning about daylight, I found Queequeg's arm thrown over me in the most loving and affectionate manner. You had almost thought I had been his wife" (25).

Leslie Fiedler is among the critics who see Ishmael's relationship to Queequeg as a representation of "the redemptive love of man and man" (370).[14] In this whaling tale where women are left on the shore, the homoerotic cast to Ishmael and Queequeg's association is an instance in which sexuality deconstructs rather than constructs whiteness. Unlike the captivity and criminal narratives of the eighteenth and early nineteenth centuries or the antimiscegenationist subtext of *The Last of the Mohicans*, *Moby-Dick* employs no white female to represent white sexual purity, to produce future generations of a "superior" race, or to define the ideal white identity as male. Instead, its narrator, Ishmael, is feminized and becomes the "wife" of Queequeg. Degendered, he enters into a homoerotic union with a "spouse" of another race, an act that defies both the championed heterosexual norm of white identity and the racial purity represented through the ideal of white femininity. The relationship of Ishmael and Queequeg thus transgresses two key norms of whiteness: heterosexuality and racial purity. Ishmael becomes an alternative representation of white sexuality, restoring it to its erotic origins and divorcing it from its function as a surrogate for social, sexual, and racial values.

Over time, Ishmael's encounters with Queequeg and others color not only his perspective but even his physical appearance. Later in the novel, a tattooed Ishmael describes how he kept information on the size of a whale skeleton:

> The skeleton dimensions I shall now proceed to set down are copied verbatim from my right arm, where I had them tattooed; as in my wild wanderings at that period, there was no other secure way of preserving such valuable statistics. But as I was crowded for space, and wished the other parts of my body

to remain a blank page for a poem I was then composing—at least, what untattooed parts might remain—I did not trouble myself with the odd inches. (451)

The now-tattooed Ishmael has left the insularity of his white skin for a new body of meaning, in which whiteness is just one of many elements. Unlike figures such as Hawkeye and Alice Munro, he represents a white identity proud not to be visibly "pure" and unafraid of being marked as a hybrid of many racial and cultural influences. An extraordinary literary achievement, he suggests an alternative way for whiteness to be in a multicultural and multiracial America. By making Ishmael physically akin to Queequeg, whose tattooing makes him "a wondrous work in one volume" (480–81), Melville deepens the parallel between the two and further obscures their racial difference. More significant, however, he makes Ishmael a new "text," one very different from those mentioned in "Extracts." The lone survivor of the *Pequod*'s voyage, he symbolizes the beginning of new traditions of knowledge and knowing. New literacies will be required to read him, ones whose grammars and lexicons derive from racial and cultural tolerance.

It is noteworthy that *Moby-Dick* takes place on the open seas, for its democratic vision seems antithetical to the social vision of land conquest and removals that dominated so much of America's frontier literature of the period.[15] As Leslie Fiedler observes, "The whole movement of the book is from land to sea, from time to timelessness; and Melville succeeds in converting all that is provincial in his subject into the universal by removing it from the land-bound world of history back toward the oceanic" (382). This moving is effected through the agency of a singular, eccentric craft sailing from New Bedford, a city whose very variety reflects American diversity: "[A]ctual cannibals stand chatting at street corners; . . . besides the Feegeeans, Tongatabooans, Erromanggoans, Pannangians, and Brighggians, and, besides the wild specimens of whaling-craft which unheeded reel about the streets, you will see other sights still more curious, certainly more comical[,] . . . scores of green Vermonters and New Hampshire men, all athirst for gain and glory in the fishery" (31). The variety of New Bedford and the *Pequod* are Melville's most eloquent denunciations of one group asserting its racial identity as a national norm, its superiority among a land of varied peoples.

Moby-Dick is far more than the tale of a crazed monomaniac's quest to conquer a white whale representing all that frustrates him; it is also a cautionary tale of the dangers posed to American democracy by blindly pursuing an ideology of whiteness that seeks to make one group the masters of others. It daringly questions the "progress," the "superiority," the privileging of whiteness accomplished though arbitrary systems of classification, fraudulent sciences, erroneous portraits, and biased canonization. In 1851 it broached what is only beginning to be forthrightly discussed today—the need for whiteness to be named and deconstructed. Examinations such as Melville's were rare, however. In virtually every aspect of American culture at this time, the primacy and idealization of whiteness were mass-produced and mass-marketed, and its establishment as an unrecognized norm was at once very subtle and very complete.

4

Hiding Whiteness
in Plain Sight

. . . but America was America to us. We knew no
distinction of West and East. By rights there ought to
have been buffaloes and red Indians charging up and
down Broadway.

—*Jacob Riis*

WHEN TRAVELING in Cajamarca, Peru, I met a young boy
who wanted to know where I lived. Africa? he asked. No, I
replied, the United States. He looked at me quizzically and
started laughing. They don't have people like you there, he
responded. His laughter and beliefs reminded me of how thor-
oughly whiteness is equated with Americanness. This specious
synonymity has been accomplished by means of a vast promulgation of images through an extensive network of media.
When did this promulgation begin on a large scale? At what
point in American history were there enough institutions capable of mass-producing and widely disseminating notions of
a white ideology not only within the United States but also
abroad? What was the content of those popular images? A body

of writings that suggest answers to these questions are the narratives of early-twentieth-century European immigrants. Their autobiographies provide some of the clearest profiles of the cultural instruments that shaped and spread an ideology of whiteness in a multiracial America. The written recollections of those who were not yet American reveal the constructed nature of whiteness through recounting life stories of white-skinned peoples who had to learn the privileging of whiteness and its synonymity with American identity.

It is easy to interpret the genre of immigrant autobiography solely as stories of acculturation and overlook its usefulness in illuminating those turn-of-the-century tools of cultural hegemony that solidified notions of whiteness in the United States. One work widely regarded as emblematic of the genre at this time exemplifies how immigrant narrative may be used to discover the ways in which seemingly nonracial institutions and rituals were in actuality part of a multifaceted cultural matrix that was diagramming and urging conformity to a white ideal.

•

In *The Promised Land* (1911), Mary Antin, a Russian Jew born in Polotzk (Plotzk), chronicles her migration to the United States when conditions for Jews worsened in eastern Europe prior to World War I. Her autobiography is seen by some as the quintessential work of immigrant narrative written during the early twentieth century. The English writer and social philosopher Horace Bridges characterized her book as "one of those masterpieces which, under the guise of a record of individual experience, bring before us the full pulsating life of ages and nations" (ix). In her story, Antin incorporates themes, hopes, and desires articulated in many immigrant life stories of the time. Her chronicle follows a common arc that begins by detailing life in the homeland and the decision to migrate, moves on to describe experiences of arrival and acculturation, and ends with reflections on what it means to be an American. She sums up this arc in her introduction by writing, "I was born, I have lived, and I have been made over" (xi). In that concise set of statements she captures the process of assimilation, a central concern to many early narratives, as a cursory glance at selected titles indicates: *The Making of an American* (1901), by Jacob Riis; *On Becoming an American* (1918), by Horace Bridges; *The Americanization of Edward Bok* (1920). Yet what does the process of being "made over" entail?

For each author, of course, the experience of being "made over" was unique. It was a relatively easy process for Horace Bridges, who faced no language, religious, or class barriers and was so familiar with English and American traditions that his account of being "made over" reads more like an exegesis of American culture than a narrative of migration. For writers such as Edward Bok and Jacob Riis, being "made over" meant overcoming initial poverty as well as language barriers and being able to participate fully in American culture—Bok through stewarding the creation and production of the *Ladies Home Journal* and Riis through devoting his life to revealing the horrors of urban poverty in works such as *How the Other Half Lives* (1890).

In telling their stories of transformation, immigrant auto-biographers generally defined being made into Americans broadly, as gaining the freedom to fulfill personal potential through acquiring education, economic security, and partaking in democratic processes. Within this broad definition are implicit assumptions, however, that the "real" American identity is a white, Protestant, and economically privileged one. With the exception of a few mentions of African Americans or Chinese Americans in some narratives, these autobiographies erase race in recalling their subjects' experiences yet implicitly racialize the national identity to which their subjects aspire.[1] In Mary Antin's childhood recollections, instances of this implied racialization are evident in descriptions characterizing exemplary American identity as she found it personified in the weekly program offered by the local mission, her public education, the literature she read, and her contact with "genuine" Americans. In reflecting on each, she reveals the degree to which white, Protestant, affluent, and American were blurred in her mind.

Of the local mission Antin writes:

> And there was Morgan Chapel. . . . All the children of the neighborhood, except the most rowdyish, flocked to Morgan Chapel at least once a week. This was on Saturday evening, when a free entertainment was given, consisting of music, recitations, and other parlor accomplishments. . . . We hung upon the lips of the beautiful ladies who read or sang to us. . . . We admired the miraculously clean gentlemen who sang or played. . . . Sometimes the beautiful ladies were accompanied by ravish-

ing little girls who stood up in a glory of golden curls, frilled petticoats, and silk stockings, to recite pathetic or comic pieces, with trained expression and practised gestures that seemed to us the perfection of the elocutionary art. We were all a little bit stage-struck after these entertainments; but what was more, we were genuinely moved by the glimpses of a fairer world than ours which we caught through the music and poetry; the world in which the beautiful ladies dwelt with the fairy children and the clean gentlemen. (266–67)

Morgan Chapel is illustrative of many religious and social reform institutions that attempted to ease the transition from immigrant to citizen. Here white, Protestant citizens, many of means, who were committed to the cause of spreading their religion and enacting social change, gathered weekly to enrich the lives of working-class urban residents, perhaps through musical entertainment, oratories, and planned excursions. Along with social enrichment came social values, however, and these institutions became models that suggested what types of behavior and knowledge would assist in moving into the American mainstream, in becoming "real" Americans. One result of her visits to the chapel is Antin's feeling that beyond her Jewish American world lies a better American one, and she represents its superiority through idealized images of white identity: "beautiful ladies," "clean gentlemen," and "ravishing little girls who stood up in a glory of golden curls."

The people of Morgan Chapel were not the only models of "authentic" Americans available to Antin, however; her public schooling provided others. In speaking of a special relationship with a teacher, she reflects:

> It was Miss Dillingham . . . who helped me in so many ways. . . . She invited me to tea one day, and I came in much trepidation. It was my first entrance into a genuine American household; my first meal at a Gentile—yes, a Christian—board. Would I know how to behave properly? (249)

Miss Dillingham is clearly more than an instructor of academic skills. She is a representation of the behavior and mannerisms that mark a "genuine" American: she is white, she is a Gentile, and she comes from a class caste above Antin's. In Antin's mind, these disparate elements of behavior, religion, class, and race coalesce into an American ideal.

In addition to real-life models, Antin also had the benefit of those that existed in the pages of literature. She characterizes her favorite reading matter thus:

> What books did I read . . . diligently? Pretty nearly everything that came to my hand. . . . Of these I remember with the greatest delight Louisa Alcott's stories. A less attractive series of books was of the Sunday School type. In volume after volume a very naughty little girl by the name of Lulu was always going into tempers, that her father might have opportunity to lecture her and point to her angelic little sister, Gracie, as an example of what she should be; after which they all felt better and prayed. Next to Louisa Alcott's books in my esteem were boys' books of adventure, many of them by Horatio Alger; and I read all, I suppose, of the Rollo books, by Jacob Abbot. (257)

The books Antin read created an America that was a constellation of white images, including a white, female New England childhood; a pious white cherub and her devout Protestant family; and the adventures of young, often upwardly mobile, white males.[2] Antin viewed the whole of it as simply "American" and having no particular race or class content; however, when whites are the only personifications of privilege, social mobility, economic security, and cultural refinement, experiences and products that appear race-neutral are implicitly racialized.

Antin's autobiography is instructive in that it illustrates the conflation of whiteness, Protestantism, and privilege. Because the education, cultural enrichment, and social mobility she desired as alternatives to urban poverty were personified through Miss Dillingham, the characters of Louisa May Alcott, and the reformers present at Morgan Chapel, a vision of America in which only privileged whites characterize authentic Americanness pervades her life story. This vision is the direct result of a monoracializing of American experience in which racial barriers generally prohibited nonwhites from teaching in schools with predominantly white student populations, be they native-born or immigrant; in which literature representing nonwhite experiences was rarely widely disseminated; and in which missionary organizations did not commonly employ nonwhites to minister to the needs of the urban poor. Thus, few alternative representations existed to counter the persistent linking of whiteness to a desirable social norm.

The Promised Land is the story of one woman's experience;

but as Horace Bridges observed, it gave voice to the sensibilities of many seeking to enter that "fairer world." Its content is repeated in many works of this genre, and as such, it reveals how Antin and millions like her came to envision the "genuine" America as a nation peopled by privileged, white, Protestant Americans. But how did Antin, a resident of a multiracial, multicultural, working-class Boston neighborhood of Jewish and African Americans that she characterized as "bearded Arlington Street" and "wool-headed Arlington Street" (260), come to define American identity so narrowly? What cultural agents impressed her imagination and those of others?

At the time Antin wrote, the production of ideas and products contributing to popular conceptions of a "fairer world" was occurring on an unprecedented scale in the United States. New technology, new forms of mass entertainment, and a desire to codify definitions of American identity in response to a rise in immigration spawned myriad agents extolling the virtues of a white American ideal. Since an exhaustive investigation of all the movies, newspapers, novels and stories, radio broadcasts, museums, world's fairs, etiquette books, public school curricula, and social reform institutions that contributed to this enterprise would be impossible in a single volume, I take a representative sampling of agents suggested by Antin's own words—world's fairs, settlement houses, public schools, and etiquette books—to provide a sense of how various vehicles explicitly and implicitly maintained notions of an idealized whiteness.

"We Were Genuinely Moved By the Glimpses of a Fairer World"

In the late nineteenth and early twentieth centuries, one did not have to look far for representations of the "fairer world" Antin imagined beyond her own. The turn of the century was rich with publicly touted assertions of what constituted the ideal American world, and implicit in these assertions was the whiteness of this world. The merchandising of whiteness began in earnest during this period, and one of the most effective means of displaying its desirable traits, forms, and values and of promoting their adoption was the world's fair. Beginning in the United States in 1876, these orchestrated representations of what constituted a "fairer world" were regular features of the American landscape. Cities as varied as Philadelphia, Chicago, Seattle, New Orleans, and New York were among the many host sites for world's fairs, and total attendance exceeded, by conservative estimates, one hundred million people. Taking their lead from previous international expositions held abroad, such as London's Crystal Palace (1851) and the Paris Exposition (1889), these fairs were meant to showcase the best of American arts, crafts, and industry. They were designed to be celebrations of United States ascendancy not only as an economic and industrial power but also as a seat of culture.[3] Further, at a time of enormous social change in American society, the fairs were one means of providing common national identity to competing societal segments.

Of the period that saw the rise of world's fairs in the United States, Robert Rydell, a noted historian of exhibitions, writes:

Increasing industrialization and cyclical industrial depressions, beginning in 1873, resulted in frequent outbursts of open class warfare. The urgency expressed in social reform movements and in the flood of utopian writings at the century's end reflected the country's unsettled condition. Adding to the worries of the times was the discovery of unfathomable multiplicity in the universe. All these concerns gave troubled American Victorians an intense drive to organize experience. . . . To alleviate the intense and widespread anxiety that pervaded the United States, the directors of the expositions offered millions of fairgoers an opportunity to reaffirm their collective national identity in an updated synthesis of progress and white supremacy that suffused the blueprints of future perfection offered by the fairs.[4]

Rydell's observation that there was a discernible link between the fairs' showcasing American progress and manifesting white supremacy is key. Often this dual content was evident in the very layout of the fairs. At the 1876 Philadelphia Centennial Exposition, for example, "Displays from around the world were organized in the Main Building according to race." "France and Colonies" represented the Latin races; "England and Colonies" the Anglo-Saxon races; the "German Empire," Austria, and Hungary the Teutonic races. While exhibits from Mexico, Brazil, China, and Japan were also present, the United States, England, France, and Germany were given the most prominent display areas (*ATWF*, 21–22). Other fair elements may have shown a less overt race awareness but nonetheless conveyed racialized notions of what was truly American. Included among the crafts displayed at the Philadelphia fair, for instance, was a bedstead manufactured by Nelson, Matter, & Company, furniture makers, and described by scholar David Scobey in his essay "What Shall We Do with Our Walls?": "Its headboard rose nearly eighteen feet, crowned with a carved American eagle; its massive, Renaissance-revival frame contained some half-dozen sculptural niches which displayed such culture-heroes as Columbus and Gutenberg . . . a statue of the goddess Columbia . . . her symbolic mate, George Washington, presiding under an elaborate Gothic arch" (in Rydell and Gwinn, 87). The triumvirate of the goddess Columbia, George Washington, and Gutenberg links abstract notions of liberty, nation, and technology to visible white personages, thereby coloring with race ideas of democracy and progress. Over the course of exposition history, more than bedsteads would accomplish the same end, as the racial content of successive fairs became increasingly blatant.

At the Philadelphia exposition, the emphasis was on American industry. At the next major world's fair in the United States, the emphasis was clearly on American culture. The 1893 Chicago World's Columbian Exposition, popularly (and as we will soon see, appropriately) known as the White City, sought to represent America as an emergent world power and a civilized nation. No longer colonies or provinces, the United States was a leading industrial nation desirous of displaying its own "high" culture. Historian David Burg captures the magnitude of the White City's impact on the American cultural imagination when he describes the various materials it inspired:

The White City's life was brief but legendary. It inspired hundreds of publications—catalogs, photographic albums, speeches, essays, novels. . . . A merely cursory investigation reveals that the World's Columbian Exposition evoked far more commentary than any exposition in history. (xi)

The symbols and images engendered by or present at the exposition did not mirror the nation's diversity, however, but rather advocated a white nation in which racial difference was contained or erased. Modern transport enabled people from many different geographic areas of the United States—indeed, from many different areas of the world—to come and feast on interpretations of what it meant to be American and, by extension, that being authentically American meant being white.

In true American fashion, definitions of whiteness at the White City were constructed against definitions of nonwhiteness. Historian Reid Badger cites some examples of this symbiosis:

The Louisiana Building contained a Creole kitchen, antebellum style, complete with "snowily turbaned and aproned colored cooks and waiters, and superintended by young ladies of Caucasian blood, representing the beauty and hospitality of that Grand Commonwealth." (104)

The Bureau of Indian Affairs and the Ethnological Bureau prepared extensive exhibits for the Government Building on Indian customs and life in North and South America, in which visitors could see contrasted "the red man as a savage wrapped in a blanket, and his child in the dress of civilization, endeavoring to master benignant mysteries." (105)

These exhibits reinforced traditional racial conceptions in which whiteness was privileged against a backdrop of nonwhite servility and primitivism. The layout of the fair itself further expressed this contrast. Accompanying the formal pavilions the fair devoted to American arts and industry were sections devoted purely to popular entertainment. At the Chicago fair, this section was called the Midway Plaisance and catered to a fascination with "exotica" or, in other words, to white voyeurism.

In the Midway, visitors were treated to American-imagined re-creations of, among others, a Dahomey village and Cairo, Egypt; or they might witness the gyrations of "Fatima, an oriental type of beauty." Since few fairgoers had access to the actual places or persons, the caricatures here might as well have been reality. A program of weekly events offered spectators "daily ethnographical exhibitions": "Free Concerts of Typical Music by Representatives of Every Race in Native Costumes and with Native Instruments"; "Boat Races by all Nations, Savage and Civilized"; and "Some Sensational Feature—War, Religious and Ceremonial Dances by Savage Tribes" (World's Columbian Exposition Program, 1893, National Museum of American History). Reid Badger describes the Midway as ". . . a major factor in the rising attendance figures which the world's fair enjoyed beginning in late June" (106). The Midway's attractions essentially made nonwhite cultures into sideshows. While many came to see the displays of arts and industries in the formal pavilions of the fair, many more came to see the Midway's depictions of exotic "aberrance." There viewers were provided with racial notions or had their existing notions affirmed. The Midway was just one half of a system constructing a concept of whiteness, however. The other half included the displays in pavilions devoted to "legitimate" art and culture.

While the Midway assembled exoticism, the Art Palace, for example, assembled what were then esteemed to be paintings and sculptures representing American ascendancy to the highest levels of refined civilization. Organizers of the fair intended for the paintings and sculptures displayed to show the United States's evolution into a country with its own body of "serious" art. Gathered there were images of nature, such as Winslow Homer's *Sunlight on the Coast* (1890); portrayals of myths, such as Edwin A. Abbey's *Galahad Brought to Arthur's Court* (ca. 1890–1893); portrayals of monuments to technological advances, such as Frank M. Boggs's *The Brooklyn Bridge, New York* (ca. 1889); and portraits of human subjects in a variety of lights. Though often seen as a counterpoint to the exotic "otherness" of the Midway, images in the Art Palace actually recapitulated in "high" art racial values identical to those present in the former. Rather than allow visitors to infer white superiority while gazing on the spectacle of nonwhiteness, the Art Palace provided image after image that outrightly conveyed whiteness not only as superior but as the legitimate racial identity of the United States.

Many of the pictures gathered in the palace took for their subjects, events in American history from the colonial era to the time of the exposition. Scenes of early America, the West, the antebellum South, and emerging cosmopolitan centers solidified epochs that had become key parts of American mytho-history: settlement, westward expansion, the "peculiar institution," and industrialism. Two works from Edward Moran's series of paintings devoted to United States shipping history, for example, symbolically capture the myth of American conquest and expansion, at the nation's beginning and in the nineteenth century. *The First Ship Entering New York Harbor* (1892) depicts a Native American perched on a rock, gazing at an oncoming vessel. The second serves as a coda to the history foreshadowed in the first: *The White Squadron's Farewell Salute to Commodore John Ericsson* (ca. 1891) renders the *Baltimore*, a prized armed cruiser that represented the United States's emerging turn-of-the-century naval power.

Other paintings included in the Art Palace consisted of landscapes imagining a pristine America, simple and agrarian, which amid Victorian industrial and social change harked back to a less complex past. An overwhelming number of the pictures were portraits of white figures in a variety of attitudes, from the ordinary—as in Gari Melchers's *Married* (ca. 1892), depicting a young couple in modest garb as they wed—to the genteel—as portrayed in Jules L. Stewart's *On the Yacht Namouna, Venice, 1890* (1890), rendering a set of bourgeois couples lounging on the deck of a yacht. The range of poses and class situations in these paintings designed to showcase what was American, along with the consistency of the subjects' race, ultimately defined the United States as a land peopled by whites. What depictions of nonwhites were present in the Art Palace showed them as exceptions to a pervasive white norm. Native Americans were often contained in naturalistic backdrops, symbolizing nostalgia for a vanished American past, as exemplified by George de Forest Brush's *The Indian and the Lily* (1887). African Americans were presented either as indigent, as in Alfred Kappes's depiction of a destitute woman in *Tattered and Torn* (1886), or as nonthreatening children, as in J. G. Brown's *A Card Trick* (ca. 1880s).

The images of white women collected in the Palace are also telling, for they represent the increasing confinement of women to the domestic sphere. White women of the upper classes were consciously posed seated in parlors, as in Frank W. Benson's *Portrait of a Lady in White* (1889). Working-class women were shown in agrarian scenes for the most part, as in Eanger Irving Couse's *Milking Time* (1892) and Guy Rose's *Potato Gatherers* (1891). In many of the portraits, women appeared in domestic settings.[5] J. T. Harwood's *Preparing Dinner* (1891) shows a woman seated at a table peeling apples; Alice D. Kellogg's *The Mother* (1889) portrays a woman preparing to nurse a child; and John Singer Sargent's 1890 *Portrait of a Boy* (Homer Saint Gauden's) is a painting of sculptor Augustus Saint-Gaudens's son in which the son appears seated in the center of the portrait, his mother in the background reading to him. The presence of white women as members of an exploited industrial working class is virtually erased in these artistic representations. On the whole, these images of women, while possibly containing more complex thematic elements, when gathered in exhibition for casual viewing reinforced the notion of women in the background, relegated to menial or domestic spheres, a portrayal in marked contrast to the white female presence that brought the Woman's Building into existence or that was so vital to the fund-raising and organizational activities of the fair.[6]

The vision of the United States that emerged in the Art Palace was essentially one of a white nation with clearly defined gender and class roles; a vision in which those who were non-white were relegated to primitivism, nostalgia, or spectacle. The exhibition was the natural consequence of an ideology of whiteness that formed in the period of colonial settlement and evolved through the Revolutionary period and the nineteenth-century era of industrialism. Looking at these pictures and their contrasting elements in the Midway, visitors were continually treated to images that racialized notions of American progress, civilization, and national definition and that increasingly associated whiteness with class privilege.

What the exposition in Chicago did to set forth conceptions of whiteness other expositions continued. Many had equivalent Midway sections, but increasingly, the fairs included ethnological and anthropological exhibitions that employed erroneous science to endorse the supremacy of whiteness. At the 1904 Louisiana Purchase Exposition in St. Louis, W. J. McGee, the head ethnologist of the Bureau of American Ethnology, with the aid of missionary and amateur anthropologist Samuel Phillips Verner, mounted an exhibition on the evolution of mankind that included live subjects such as the Pygmy Ota Benga, whom Verner brought from what was then Belgian Congo. More than just a display meant to titillate, this presentation essayed to give scientific credence to the "natural" supremacy of whiteness. Verner's grandson, Phillips Verner Bradford, describes the logic behind the exhibition:

> But even a Buffalo Bill could display Indians, just as a P. T. Barnum could exhibit freaks. [W. J.] McGee's aims were more serious. He aspired to raise anthropology above the amateurish sideshows and ragtag miscellanies that had gone under the name at previous fairs. He wanted to be exhaustively scientific in his demonstration of the stages of human evolution. Therefore, in St. Louis, he required "darkest blacks" to set off against "dominant whites" and members of the "lowest known culture" to contrast with "its highest culmination." (Bradford and Blume, 94–95)

McGee's display gave the illusion of scientific evidence to racial ideology, and it continued to establish the supremacy of whiteness in contrast to nonwhiteness. Expositions in San Francisco in 1915 and San Diego in 1915–1916 repeated these contrasts. Increasingly, the fairs reiterated a construct of racial evolution that placed whiteness at the apex and employed a wide range of cultural spectacle as evidence: ethnological exhibits of Native Americans, Chinese, Filipinos, and Africans; the crass stereotypical entertainment of the midways; fine arts idealizing the normativeness of whiteness; and even material novelties, such as miniature cotton bales sold by ex-slaves who had grown the cotton.[7]

Over time, the racial themes of the fairs became more explicit. One indication of this trend was the presence of eugenics exhibits. As Robert Rydell explains,

> Beginning with the 1915 San Francisco Panama-Pacific International Exposition, American eugenicists became active in the nation's exhibition culture. . . . By the turn of the century, and certainly by the second decade of the century, world's fairs were well established as one of the most effective vehicles for transmitting ideas of scientific racism from intellectual elites to millions of ordinary Americans. . . . Because world's fairs provided "visible proof" in an age that prized "teaching by object lessons," exhibitions gained authority and were often regarded as "world's universities." (*World of Fairs*, 39–40)

Employment of visual spectacle and technical media to promulgate the tenets of eugenics took many forms. Eugenicists at some fairs mounted morality pageants, which were in essence cautionary tales of the dangers of "race degeneracy." One particularly unique manifestation was the "Fitter Families for Future Firesides Contest," which ostensibly was a means of bringing to the public knowledge of how to improve family health but in actuality was a means of transmitting the racial doctrines of the eugenics missions.[8]

The first of such contests was held at the 1920 Kansas Free Fair. The success of this exhibition led to similar contests at fairs in Arkansas, Texas, Georgia, Oklahoma, Michigan, and Massachusetts, as well as in Philadelphia. These sorts of exhibitions reached a pinnacle with the 1940 New York World's Fair, in which officials held a "typical American family contest" to publicize the fair:

> To help local civic leaders judge contest winners, world's fair authorities circulated a questionnaire that included "racial

origin" as one of the categories to be considered. World's fair authorities also made clear that they hoped each family unit selected would "consist of parents and two children." The results were predictable. "Typical" American families were native-born white Americans. (Rydell, *World of Fairs*, 57)

The "Fitter Families" contests provided a unique twist to the privileging of whiteness: They moved the values implicit in this ideology from the arena of spectacle and made whiteness a participatory event. Fairgoers were no longer just onlookers observing visual representations of white superiority; now, interactively, they could imagine themselves as personifications of this ideal.

The world's fairs accomplished a tremendous amount of socialization. Under the guise of entertainment, they carried an ideology of whiteness not only to millions within the United States but also to a global audience. Through art, ethnological displays, eugenics contests, and souvenirs, expositions privileged whiteness and justified the sentiment that the governance and development of a multiracial nation should primarily serve the interests of one racial group. They were examples of overt articulations of the primacy of whiteness; but this primacy was also rearticulated in numerous less overt fashions. What expositions accomplished on a large scale other cultural agents, such as settlement houses, accomplished in more common venues.

"We Hung upon the Lips of the Beautiful Ladies who Read or Sang to Us"

The white, Protestant, middle-class Morgan Chapel volunteers who provided Saturday-evening entertainment for Antin's neighborhood exemplified participants in a progressive movement for social reform. In the latter half of the nineteenth century, this blossoming movement increased its advocacy for causes as varied as decreased workdays, improved work-safety conditions, reform of juvenile law, the end of child labor, and a solution to urban poverty. Another calling of this movement was the acculturation of newly arriving immigrants, and it is in this mission that the ways in which whiteness was conflated with particular class values are evident.

Historian Anne Boylan describes who were the initial instruments of this movement and how they organized their activities:

> [T]he first houses of refuge, reform schools, orphanages, old-age homes, and modern hospitals were begun by groups of men and women who formed voluntary societies and raised donations from among friends, relatives, acquaintances, and strangers. (2)

Though not stated outright, the ability to raise funds from relatives, acquaintances, and strangers implies a class community of some means. Generally during this period, organizers of reform came from the middle and upper classes. As a result, the content of many of their reform activities reflected their class values. In the autobiographical reflections of two such relief workers, the ways in which institutions that seemingly had no race or class agenda implicitly conveyed notions that cemented a race concept with the values of a particular class can be noted. Jane Addams and Lillian Wald, founders of Hull-House and the House on Henry Street, respectively, left in their memoirs indications that even settlement houses were not immune to idealizing whiteness and making it synonymous with American identity.

Jane Addams was the daughter of John Huy Addams, a Quaker immigrant who came to Illinois from Pennsylvania and made a substantial fortune through holdings in railroads, banks, and insurance. Jane benefited from her father's wealth but, after a formal education and trips abroad to Europe, found that the opportunities to apply her training and gifts were constrained by gender. Hull-House allowed her to put her education and idealism to practical use.[9] Along with her friend Ellen Starr, she purchased the former home of Charles J. Hull, and in 1889 they renovated it and provided a community resource for those in the environment of Chicago's Halsted Street. Addams attempted to overcome "the assumption that the sheltered, educated girl has nothing to do with the bitter poverty and the social maladjustment which is all about her" (Addams, 45). Her aims were "To provide a center for a higher civic and social life; to institute and maintain educational and philanthropic enterprises; and to investigate and improve the conditions in the industrial districts of Chicago" (66).

In speaking of her work with Jewish, Italian, Irish, and German immigrant populations, Addams articulated her mission "to preserve and keep whatever of value their past life contained and to bring them in contact with a better type of Americans" (136). Addams's wording here is significant. Ethnic identity—the holidays, cultural rituals, language, dress, cooking, folklore, and religious practices of a people—was consigned to being of the past, part of a life to be left as one advanced toward a future identity that would be secured through adopting the practices and values of a "better type" (read middle- and upper-class white) of Americans. While "German Night," "Italian Night," and "Irish Night" were regular events devised by Hull-House to cater to the ethnic diversity of its community, these nights were essentially ethnic moments existing against the continuity of a white, Protestant, bourgeois norm. Their placement amid an institutional program pervaded by an ethos of acculturation cast them as cultural respites along the journey to becoming American.

In its early years during the turn of the century, everything from home furnishings to the content of the various clubs at Hull-House reaffirmed a standard of white privilege, as did the absence of any racial diversity. African Americans, for example, were excluded from the settlement community due to sentiment that their presence would discourage other immigrant groups from partaking of the house's services. The source of such sentiment is not made clear in Addams's writings, but the absence of African Americans amid a community of white immigrants and offspring of immigrants subtly validated notions of a monoracial American identity and missed an opportunity to facilitate cross-racial awareness.[10] Hull-House was by no means a consciously segregated enterprise, but a hierarchy of purpose to serve those with white skins first is evident.[11] White-skinned European immigrants were thus introduced to the benefit of skin color as an aid to social and economic access, and they could measure their progress against the status of those who did not have white skin. The ideology of whiteness that privileged their skin color camouflaged differences in class, language, ethnicity, and culture between their own experiences and those of the "genuine" Americans they sought to emulate.

Every detail of Hull-House reiterated white privilege, even the furnishings. In describing how she selected accoutrements for the house, Addams wrote:

> We furnished the house as we would have furnished it were it in another part of the city, with the photographs and other impedimenta we had collected in Europe, and with a few bits of family mahogany. . . . We believed that the Settlement may logically bring to its aid all those adjuncts which the cultivated man regards as good and suggestive of the best life of the past. (57)

One of these adjuncts included an art studio decorated with originals and reproductions of famous American and European works, some of which actually had been on display at the Chicago exposition. Their presence reaffirmed western Europeans as the true progenitors of American identity and further disseminated the sensibilities of the white middle and upper classes to those seeking to become citizens of the United States. In an institution where many came to learn how to be "better" Americans, these materials subtly dictated what constituted authentic and sanctioned American cultural values. They implicitly rearticulated an ideology that those who contributed to American history and cultural development came from one idealized racial, cultural, and class group having western European origins.

The standards implicit in the artwork and furnishings were also affirmed through the house's activities. Addams describes one of the earliest events, in which a Miss Starr "started a reading party in George Eliot's 'Romola,' which was attended by a group of young women who followed the wonderful tale with unflagging interest" (61). She goes on to relate another instance in which a resident,

> a charming old lady . . . gave five consecutive readings from Hawthorne to a most appreciative audience, interspersing the magic tales most delightfully with recollections of the elusive and fascinating author. Years before she had lived at Brook Farm as a pupil of the Ripleys, and she came to us for ten days because she wished to live once more in an atmosphere where "idealism ran high." We thus early found the type of class which through all the years has remained most popular—a combination of a social atmosphere with serious study. (61)

Neither overt nor intrusive, and certainly pleasurable, this combination of the social and the serious proved an effective means of disseminating both culture and ideology to immigrants whom Addams describes as experiencing a "curious isolation" (66). Separated from the countries, regions, and rituals that once cemented their ethnic identities and faced with the challenge of integrating a new culture into their existing ones, these newly arrived residents were a prime audience for imbibing the content and images of American life represented in its canonical literature.

Many writings contributed to Hull House's literary scene, yet all came from a single standard. Addams recalls, for instance, "one enthusiastic leader who read aloud to a club a translation of 'Antigone,' which she had selected because she believed that the great themes of the Greek poets were best suited to young people" (197). She also describes one participant's reaction to the readings of the Shakespeare Club:

> I recall that one of its earliest members said that her mind was peopled with Shakespeare characters during her long hours of sewing in a shop, that she couldn't remember what she thought about before she joined the club, and concluded that she hadn't thought about anything at all. (249)

Addams mentions other writers empowered to uplift young minds in this passage where she articulates her conception of the power of art:

> To feed the mind of the worker, to lift it above the monotony of his task, and to connect it with the larger world, outside of his immediate surroundings, has always been the object of art, perhaps never more nobly fulfilled than by the great English bard. Miss Starr has held classes in Dante and Browning for many years and the great lines are conned with never failing enthusiasm. (249)

In addition to the inspiration and adventure of literature, the selection of works presented here offers discernible racial representations. White features are trumpeted as the ideal of physical beauty; almost all the actors in this canon are white; and nonwhite figures, when not completely absent, are caricatured. Since the readings and lectures were envisioned as providing examples of characteristics and qualities to be emulated in real life, the clubs fostered a narrow, race-specific conception of desirable society that erased the actual complexity and variety of literature and history. In so doing, they became small mechanisms conveying an ideology asserting the primacy and universality of whiteness, however benignly, to a variety of groups seeking to participate fully in American culture.

Hull-House is not the only example of an institution that was serving a community and at the same time socializing it to particular race and class notions. The House on Henry Street shared many similarities with Hull-House, from its social mission to the insinuated transference of values and ideals. Begun by Lillian D. Wald and Mary M. Brewster in 1895, it attempted to address the economic and social challenges that faced New York's recently arrived immigrants and industrial working classes. In opening her memoirs, Wald describes her and Brewster's mission "to live in the neighborhood as nurses, identify ourselves with it socially, and, in brief, contribute to it our citizenship" (8–9). Again we have a model in which members of the middle and upper classes not only lend assistance in day-to-day sustenance to those less fortunate than themselves but also become living models of an idealized white, privileged, and Protestant American identity to which white-skinned immigrants might aspire. The House on Henry Street grew over the years, gradually expanding to become the Henry Street Settlement and including nearby properties used for ends as varied as rooftop playgrounds, clubhouses, and a clinic.

While ministering to the needs of New York's needy, the House on Henry Street also passed on conceptions of a monoracial America to its clients. Similar to Hull House, its reading clubs contained books that articulated standards of beauty favoring white appearances or showing in demeaning or condescendingly humourous light members of other races. Many passages in Wald's memoirs reveal the content of the settlement's cultural fare. At one point she describes her attempts to "give the children stories from the Bible and the old mythologies, fairy tales, and lives of heroes"(87). In another similar passage Wald indicates that reading matter was chosen not just to entertain but also to shape young minds. She notes that children of the settlement were "given instruction in the selection of books before they are old enough to take out their cards in the public libraries," and that "Once a week, on Friday afternoon, when there are no lessons to be prepared, [the] study-room is reserved for these smallest readers. The books are selected with reference to their tastes and attainments" (103). Among the books Wald mentions the settlement as owning are "The Life of Alexander Hamilton" and "The Life of Joan of Arc." These biographies of famous persons passed along standards for what visions and figures were thought worthy of admiration. Their qualities of heroism and intellect are inextricably tied to their appearance, particularly when no racial alternative is offered. Frederick Douglass's autobiography (a work still in circulation) and the well-documented story of Harriet Tubman, for example, were never offered as symbols of bravery, fortitude, and concern for the greater good. Even if one accepts such exclusion as benign omission, it is an omission rooted in a set of values which imply that only whites figured in any important way in human civilization. The effect of this exclusion, regardless of conscious intent, was to foster a glorification of the white race and an erasure of the presence and contributions of others. The sanctioned annals through which the dominant class in American society disseminated history, civilization, and art were part of a larger hegemony that consistently articulated the normativeness and superiority of whiteness to generation after generation who studied them.

The literary activities of the House on Henry Street were augmented by social clubs that often vivified prototypes of whiteness found in literature. The drama club, for example, performed "serious work" in addition to the ethnic pageants that were common. Shakespeare and other standards of the western European canon were represented through readings given in honor of the birthdays of famous writers. Wald recalls:

> Ellen Terry, of imperishable charm, gave Shakespearean readings on the poet's birthday, and Sarah Cowell Le Moyne gave the readings from Browning on his day. Ibsen and Shaw and Dunsany have been interpreted, and distinguished professionals have found pleasure in acting before audiences at once critical and appreciative. (188)

The foregoing discussion is by no means meant as a critique of the content of these clubs. It is meant only to suggest that such an exclusive content unpremeditatedly advocated the privileging of one group's antecedents, creations, and values. Such content reinforced the conception that history consists only of events concerned with western Europe and its diaspora, and that art and culture are meaningful only when they express the vision of Europeans of the privileged classes. Particularly in the United States, this conception goes very much against historical and cultural realities, in which many experiences have constituted the national landscape. This variety of traditions found no validation in a culture that subscribed to an ideology of whiteness that defined colonial settlement as "discovery," the taking of Native American and Mexican land as "manifest destiny," and the subordination of ethnic identity to a white norm as "the great melting pot." Further the diversity of American aesthetics found no validation in an ideology that valued written expression over oral and thereby devalued as "primitive" or "quaint" the rich, expressive legacies of Native American and African American cultures.

The transmission of an ideology of whiteness that was unwittingly facilitated through the House on Henry Street's programs took place against a settlement-house backdrop that sanctioned racial exclusion. As with Hull-House, initially African Americans were not allowed the benefits of Wald's mission; the House on Henry Street was de facto a segregated institution. At one point in her writing, Wald describes a "race woman" who challenged her to address the needs of the African American poor and working class. Wald was sympathetic, and she describes her diligent work (along with others) to "establish a branch of the settlement on the west side of the city in that section known as San Juan Hill" (162). Called Lincoln House, this institution was to bring the objectives of the House on Henry Street to African American residents of the far west side of what is now upper midtown Manhattan. The establishment of Lincoln House did not mitigate the effects of segregation on the white residents whom the House on Henry Street served, however. The erasure of another race's presence from an institution that as much as addressing day-to-day needs, formed visions of what genuine American culture was, benignly imprinted a white-skin-only version of this culture in the minds of those who had newly arrived to partake of the American enterprise. If all America were white, as the books, clubs, and models provided by the settlements indicate, then white-skinned immigrants had already been granted a measure of social standing based on their skin color and their ability to distance themselves from an undesirable racial Other.

The settlement houses undeniably accomplished great good in lessening the difficulties of moving from one culture to the next and in easing the burden of economic privation. On another level, however, they unwittingly strengthened prevailing conceptions of the ideal racial identity. For white ethnic immigrants in particular, they taught the myth of a classless American society in which all were accorded the same potential for mobility as long as they were phenotypically white. They taught that, regardless of class, by approximating certain standards of belief and behavior, skin color could be parlayed into an asset advancing a transformation into "authentic" Americanness. What is unique about settlement houses and their function in furthering constructions of whiteness is that they conveyed ideological values in the course of everyday activities: learning to sew not ethnic garb but clothes deemed appropriate by a white privileged class; learning that cooking ethnic meals was not quite as healthy as cooking meals generally created by this class;[12] learning the manners and presentations that white, privileged American society thought standard. The combining of these prosaic activities with distinct race and class values made the idealization of whiteness part of the mundane, the common, and de-emphasized any obvious racial or class ideology. A specific system of values was recast as simply being American, and the ways in which this system excluded groups who did not have white skin or taught participants in the settlement houses to devalue these groups became imperceptible.

"This Hundred-fold Miracle Is Common to the Schools in Every Part of the United States Where Immigrants Are Received"

The settlement house provided a particular brand of education, but its resources could not match those devoted to public education, whose teachings it sought to augment. It was in the latter that the rationales behind an ideology of whiteness were taught year after year, in every grade, to millions of students.

·

In recalling her schooling, Antin fondly remembered "declaiming patriotic verses in honor of George Washington and Abraham Lincoln, with a foreign accent, indeed, but with plenty of enthusiasm" (206). In immigration gateway cities such as New York and Boston, public schools were the avenues through which those who so aspired might assimilate into American culture.[13] These schools mediated between an inherited culture and an adopted one, transforming "raw" immigrant material into "finished" white American product.

During the turn of the century, into the first quarter of the twentieth century, multiculturalism was not a component of the public education mission. Instead, schools sought to make a uniform civic body. According to *The Study of History in Schools: Report to the American Historical Association* (1899), the teaching of history should "lead the pupil to a knowledge of the fundamentals of the state and society of which he is a part, to an appreciation of his duties as a citizen" (American Historical Association, 74). As the report continues, it comments on the value of studying the colonial period, and it becomes clear that the history it urges as a model for instilling civic pride is one that champions English expansion in North America:

> The period is especially interesting if viewed as a chapter in the expansion of England, a chapter in the story of the struggle between the nations of western Europe for colonies, commerce, and dominion. It must be viewed, too, as a time when the spirit of self-sufficiency and self-determination was growing,—a spirit which accounts for the Revolution and for the dominating vigor of the later democracy. (American Historical Association, 74)

The committee's report stresses the primacy of European experience in the Americas and implies that such primacy is the result of destiny. The qualities of "self-sufficiency" and "self-determination" are enlisted to mitigate a violent history of conquest and explain the inevitable European dominance of North America. Erased are the histories and presence of other groups, who become no more than squatters to be vacated once the spoils of "dominion" are secured by colonial competitors. The history instruction suggested here leaves the impression that only Europeans have figured significantly in the development of the United States and justifies the exclusion of others from the historical record to be studied by all who were seeking to become American. A "whites-only" view of history that equates Americanness with whiteness is the ultimate result.

Replacing the variety of American history with the story of one people in effect privileged the antecedents and actions of one racial group without specifically naming race. The broader curricula adopted by many public schools did the same. In outlining what he saw as necessary subject matter for the New York City public schools to teach, William H. Maxwell, the city superintendent, included the following:

> [T]he predominance of study of English—a most necessary provision in a city whose population is so largely foreign; the inculcation of a love of good literature; . . . history, not as a mere chronicle of events, but as an introduction to our "heritage" of institutions and as a reservoir of moral worth; the singing of high class music. . . . (288–89)

While it can be argued that none of the aims Maxwell recommends is explicitly racial or class based, certainly all are implicitly so. "Good literature," "history . . . as an introduction to our 'heritage' of institutions and reservoir of moral worth," and "high class music" imply categories created and sanctioned by culturally dominant and economically elite segments of white Protestant society to assert their own prominence and preserve their own interests. More important, Maxwell linked these categories to the establishment of a proper morality, thereby implying that living ethically and correctly means believing in and conforming to these values.

The tacit indoctrination of immigrant segments of the population through the public education of this time is evident in the impact of the curricular content on students. After gathering interview responses detailing the experiences of Jewish immigrants schooled in New York City, educator Stephen F. Brumberg observed,

> Nearly all informants recalled studying history that focused almost exclusively on America. It was explicitly taught as an introduction to American myths and legends, a call for the affective involvement of the learner with his or her country, and as a vehicle of moral education using great national heroes as role models. The formal study of history, which commenced in the fourth grade, conveyed the message that the torch of civilization had been passed on to the New World, and specifically to the United States, and that it was manifestly ordained. There was a decidedly Puritan-Protestant tilt to the official version of

American history, little notice was paid to Catholic-Americans and none to Jewish-Americans. (126)

In recalling his experiences with elementary education, social anthropologist Paul Wrobel exemplifies Brumberg's conclusions. In his essay "Becoming a Polish American: A Personal Point of View," Wrobel notes the difficulty he had in understanding why Americans in his studies were so different from Americans in his life:

I . . . learned that Polish names were never found in the textbooks we used in class, just in the teacher's attendance records. The roll call included names from Andrzejewski to Zakrzewski, but it never occurred to me until later why we were studying about Mr. Adams or the Green family. . . . I do feel that a very subtle lesson was taking place. We were learning, perhaps unconsciously, that our Polish names were not prized possessions. Moreover, we were beginning to develop feelings about ourselves. However subtle the lesson, we learned that perhaps there was something wrong with us for having Polish names. . . . In short, a school is a place where a child acquires an identity, a process of internalizing the values, norms, and expectations of others into his own behavior and self concept. The problem is, however, that this identity is based on what society considers desirable. And what society considers desirable is determined by what the dominant group in that society feels is best regardless of individual or cultural differences. (In Ryan, 54)

As Brumberg and Wrobel point out, for populations new to American culture the subject matter of education greatly influences self-identification. In earlier forms of instruction, curricular materials were designed to foster self-identification with what was essentially a white, Protestant, bourgeois American ideal. History, for example, was meant not to give an accurate synopsis of occurrences or thought but rather to provide academic justification for popular manifestations of an ideology of whiteness.

A further idea of the content of turn-of-the-century instruction can be gathered from Mara L. Pratt's *America's Story for America's Children* (1901). Published by D. C. Heath, the work was "intended to prepare for the regular study of history and to supplement it" (iii). Meant as a foundational complement to courses of history offered in the schools, *America's Story* exemplifies how mytho-history was conveyed to young learners. In one segment describing the French and Indian wars, for example, the language is very similar to that of the captivity narratives, in which Native Americans were cast as savage beasts preying on the innocent English:

> The Indians fell upon them like wild animals. More than sixty settlers were tomahawked. The houses were burned, and the Indians danced and yelled by the light of the fire. Only a few settlers escaped; and these, after a terrible journey, half clad, and with bare feet, dragged themselves into the fort at Albany. (31–32)

The manner in which this passage retells history recalls similar scenes from captivity narratives such as Mary Rowlandson's. No counterbalancing vision of the French and Indian wars from the perspective of Native Americans appears in Pratt's account. Subsequent descriptions of the tensions between England and France show a decidedly pro-English bias. Implicitly reiterated in this version of American history is the right of the English to the North American continent, the same vision used to justify removals and expansion of English settlements. The last paragraph in the foreword of Pratt's work reveals the degree to which this subjective vision was cast as objective fact: "The summary of the historical facts in connection with each chapter and a list of the authorities consulted, given at the end of each volume . . . serve to show how trustworthy are the stories in the books" (iv). While many sources are cited at the end of these chapters, among them Francis Parkman's *France and England in North America* (1878) and A. H. Stirling's *Torch Bearers of American History* (1895), they all repeat a vision that privileges English settlement and casts events of contestations as heroic episodes in which the ancestors of "true" Americans prevailed against all odds in their continued mission to create civilization out of an untamed frontier.

Included at the end of Pratt's history are advertisements for other educational books published by D. C. Heath, and a sampling of their blurbs reveals how many other works duplicated this view of American history. A description of Allen C. Thomas's *An Elementary History of the United States* (1901) notes,

Effort has been made to present such important phases of national growth as the difficulties and dangers of exploration, and how they were overcome by courage and perseverance; the risks and hardships of settlement, and how they were met and conquered; the independence and patriotism of the colonists, and how they triumphed. (in Pratt, Advertisements section, number 11)

Similarly, a blurb for Florence Bass's *Stories of Pioneer Life* (1901) promises accounts that

> deal chiefly with the settlement of the Ohio Valley and centre about the lives of men who, as missionaries, hunters, and settlers, were the pioneers of this section of the country. Such stories make the right kind of reading for the young American. They arouse his interest and pleasure in reading. They stir in him regard for noble lives and fix his ideals of true manhood, as well as make a solid foundation for historical study. (in Pratt, Advertisements section, number 5)

As well as providing a foundation for future historical study, history, in Bass's book, is meant to instill "true manhood," grounded in hunting, settling, and missionary work—three key tools of colonialist conquest. Again, the problematic and painful past of removals is cast as a glorification of the heroic male spirit as it expands westward and fulfills its manifest destiny.

By offering a history that casts white Protestant figures as intellectually and morally superior, that omits removals and enslavement or reenvisions them as acts of divine right or mercy, these courses essentially teach that white, English Protestants are the authentic Americans and have a greater claim to American resources than the other races contributing to the nation's creation and development. As exemplified by the New York City history curriculum and related educational materials, general education advanced a myopic record of history that justified the continued exclusion of nonwhite groups from full social enfranchisement. Experiences and thought outside the sanctioned historical annals were effectively erased in the minds of children who would grow to be American adults, and the perpetuation of a skewed perspective of American history and character was the result.

In many public schools, academic courses were complemented by what were termed "civics" courses. In the New York City public schools, these included such areas of study as "Course of Study in Manners and Conduct of Life," "Home Economics and Sewing," and "School Gardens for the Public Schools of New York City." While the academic curriculum taught what and who contributed to making American character, these other courses demarcated the qualities that would characterize that character. Manners instruction taught lessons of self-restraint and reserve, implying that the students they served did not necessarily have these characteristics; home economics taught women the standards for upholding an "American" household—what foods to cook, what types of clothing to wear and what values were appropriate to the rearing of children—and these naturally derived from a white, privileged Protestant standard. These subjects reinforced on a practical level the values that the academic courses taught in theory.

Public schooling has as one of its roles the shaping of a common social body. It aims to foster shared civic ideals that will then connect diverse peoples into a collective culture. The academic missions of most schools in the first quarter of the twentieth century, particularly those serving large groups of white-skinned European immigrants, could not conceive of this collectivity being manifest through a unified diversity. Instead, they employed a variety of subject matters to inculcate the history, values, visions, and consequence of only one segment of American society. As cultural agents, therefore, schools joined exhibitions and institutions for social reform in creating adamant cultural standards against which a variety of traditions and practices were measured. School curricula suggested a protocol of behavior designed to produce coherence in the public sphere. It fell to another cultural agent to refine this protocol and make it suitable for more intimate spheres.

"Would I Know How to Behave Properly?"

During the early twentieth century, the acquisition of manners became a pressing concern of many, and etiquette books enjoyed unprecedented popularity. When Antin took tea with her teacher Miss Dillingham, her overriding worry was whether her manners would be appropriate. Her anxiety reflects that of many new arrivals and provides one indication of why etiquette books surged in prominence during the early twentieth century. Some who made this genre so popular were, like Antin, newly arrived immigrants who thought etiquette could illuminate the way to becoming "real" Americans; others were members of the urban working class, motivated by the desire for greater class mobility; still others were from rural backgrounds and thought that proper etiquette would give them a greater cosmopolitan air.

Etiquette has a long history in the United States, though its development faced many challenges. According to historian Arthur Schlesinger,

> In struggling toward [the acquisition of manners] the American people have been hampered historically by five conditions. The first was the fact that the colonies were settled in the main by persons who in the Old World had been cut off from the usages of the best society. The second was the absence of a native hereditary aristocracy, which might, as in Europe, have served to set standards of taste and deportment; instead, a succession of classes rose to the top. A third hindrance consisted in the necessity of taming a wilderness before cultivating the graces of living, a need constantly renewed as the nation shifted westward toward the Pacific. The situation was complicated further by the incoming of . . . immigrants, people who faced all the difficulties common to the native-born as well as the additional one of having to master the unfamiliar customs of their English-speaking neighbors. (vii–viii)

Etiquette did evolve in the United States, however, and by the late nineteenth century, etiquette books were widely written and read. Many justified their content and their aims by asserting that they were essaying to civilize America, to bring it into line with European society, and to provide a system of rules that would lend social coherence. Masked by the rubric of simple "good manners," which the etiquette books attempted to make standard, were implicit comments that linked these manners to white, European, upper-class antecedents and thus racialized them and grounded them in a specific class sensibility. Within these works is a conflation of whiteness with class privilege, and etiquette was used to reinforce simultaneously both class and race ideals. Some books even went so far as to crystallize their proscriptions by contrasting "civilized" white society with "barbaric" nonwhite civilizations. This joining of race, class, and etiquette can be found in subtle form in Hallie Erminie Rives's *The Complete Book of Etiquette* (1926); a more overt example appears in Lillian Eichler's *The Customs of Mankind* (1924).

In her work Rives defines etiquette as

> a code whose object is the standardization of customs and practices with a view to social coherency. . . . [E]tiquette tends to standardize conduct, in order that the social contacts of each unit of the mannered and ceremonious world may be, so far as is humanly possible, frictionless and agreeable. (vi–vii)

The photographs that accompany Rives's text indicate that the models for the ideal standardized conduct are of one race and class. Included among the book's illustrations are photographs of a smiling, apparently upper-class, white female descending a marble staircase in wedding regalia; a white girl sitting in a nursery at a "chair and table of correct height," serving tea to her white doll; a "butler standing behind the hostess's chair after announcing 'Dinner is served, madam' "; and white patrons sitting on the deck of a trans-atlantic ocean liner. As we might expect, there is no mention of nonwhite people, though some passages cite white ethnicities other than English Protestant as they describe Jewish and Catholic traditions of marriage. Present in these descriptions is an implicit Protestant Anglo-American standard, however, revealed through language that clearly poses these practices as exceptions: "Modern Jewish weddings follow in external details many of the *general* customs" (104; italics mine) "There are, in Catholic practice, two sorts of ceremony: one is the church wedding . . . [which] resembles very closely the ceremony as conducted by a high-church *Episcopal* minister" (103; italics mine). In both descriptions, Rives characterizes religious traditions by their approximation to a presumed white, Protestant norm, and in this work that ostensibly is about codes of conduct, values citing Protestantism as the rule are subtly conveyed.

The institutions that accomplish the social coherence Rives advocates also conflate whiteness with class, as she describes them in this synopsis of where one might find appropriate models of etiquette:

> We cannot all have magnificent estates, a corps of servants, a relay of motors, first editions in priceless bindings, and a gallery of paintings for which Europe has been despoiled, but we can all use our eyes, our ears, and our minds. We can walk the streets and observe; we can visit *public libraries* and *art museums*, where awaits us the best the world affords in *written text* or *graven marble*. And through the *newspaper*, the *magazine*, and the *radio* we can bring into our homes knowledge and appreciation of what the world of taste esteems the best. (v–vi; italics mine)

Rives's observations begin with a status ideal, an upper-class vision of "magnificent estates," "corps of servants," a "relay of motors," and access to the cultural amenities provided by "first editions" and galleries. Her admonitions soon tacitly wed class values to racial values as her counsel continues. In 1926 most of the materials contained in public libraries and art museums did not reflect the multiplicity of America's racial and cultural make-up, but rather deified its western European antecedents. All but the most sensational content in mainstream newspapers, magazines, and radio broadcasts dealt with the affairs of white Americans. What on the surface seems a validation of class mores is simultaneously a validation of institutions that preserved a vision of white centrality to art, literature, culture, and current events. The scope of the sources Rives identifies provides a sense of the breadth of the hegemonic vehicles available to the privileging of whiteness. In this work that takes as its aim the promotion of general etiquette, a vision of culture and civilization as being defined solely by the traditions and practices of one race and class is clearly present.

In Rives's book, racial content is blended with class admonitions in a manner more implicit than explicit. Not so with another popular work of this genre, written by an established arbiter of American etiquette, Lillian Eichler. Her very successful *The Book of Etiquette* (1921) was designed to tell "what to do on every social occasion," and her second work, entitled *The Customs of Mankind*, was designed to tell "why you do it" (vi). In *Customs* she ventured to give what amounts to a comparative, anthropological, cross-cultural study of the history and common practices of manners, and as such, this work makes explicit the racial notions and values undergirding American philosophies of etiquette.

Eichler begins her study with a sweeping survey of the world's etiquette, encompassing the customs and practices of many different races and cultures as she sees them. All the expected stereotypes are present, as well as a centering of an etiquette ideal in a European, preferably Anglo-Saxon/German model. Though she identifies the origins of etiquette as Eastern, "Most authorities are agreed that the Orient was the seat of early culture and that manners are oriental in their origin," she quickly points out that it was not until it reached Europe that etiquette developed in earnest: "Although we find early sproutings of culture and of cultivated manners in China, Persia, Japan, and the Caliphate of Bagdad, it was not until later, in Spain, France, and other European countries, that etiquette took any serious form" (105).

The value judgments that privilege European over non-European cultures continue in the upcoming passage, quoted extensively to give a full sense of Eichler's vision:

> There are many . . . tribes in Africa. . . . There are the Pygmy tribes and the tribes of the Bantu group; . . . There are the pure Negroes and there are the tribes of Semitic and Libyan extraction. Wherever we go we find fetishism, superstition, and overwhelming fear of the unknown. . . .
>
> On Samoa Island we find a race of warriors. . . . The Polynesians, we discover, have no very definite religion, but we realize at once how grossly superstitious they are. . . .

As we journey through [Australia] we are amazed at the amount of superstition that exists. . . .

We are instantly impressed, in Japan, by the superstitions of the people. . . .

Glimpses of Europe.—Our first trip is through Spain and Portugal. We are delighted with the beautiful old gardens of Spain. . . . And we meet a caravan of colorful Spanish gipsies who dance for us the sinuous dances of their forefathers and tell us beautiful old legends that have been handed down to them through many generations.

We leave Spain with regret, but come with joy and pleasure into France. Here is the birthplace of Fashion . . . where culture made its greatest strides. . . . We are soon completely beneath the spell of beautiful old Italy. . . . Now we will visit the buried cities and contemplate the forgotten civilizations that lie beneath our feet. . . . [W]e cross the Alps into Switzerland. . . . And we see lake-dwellings that somehow take us back over the centuries and make us think of primitive days.

Now we are in Germany, land of great universities, scientists, and leaders. . . . We marvel at the examples of high caste and low caste that we see everywhere around us. There are two distinct societies—a high and a low—and they are kept strictly apart. . . . [W]e can come at last to Greece. . . . The Greeks were for centuries the nucleus of the world's best literature, architecture, thought. . . .

To conclude our European journey, we cross the North Sea into Britain. The Britons belong to the Aryan races. The term "Aryan" means noble, of good family. It is a Sanskrit word and is believed to have come from the root *ar*, to plough. . . . The Aryans, because they ploughed the ground, considered themselves the noblest of human races; and eventually the word itself came to signify that which is noble and honourable. Various European countries are included under the Aryan races. . . .

England is the land of the lord and the lady, of the vassal and the peasant, of nobility, feudalism, peasantry. It is the land of Shakespeare and of Dickens, of King Arthur and Robin Hood. There is probably no other country that has so largely influenced our own manners and customs, although we ran away from all that was England and English. (73–84)

Under the guise of discussing etiquette, Eichler's tour recapitulates racial hierarchies in which Africans were seen as the most "benighted" human species and Europeans the most "enlightened." She moves from the bottom rungs of a racial ladder, in which Pacific Islanders, Australian aborigines, and Asians have no religion, only "fetishes" and "superstitions," to the uppermost rung, where only Europeans have achieved cultivated and cultured traditions. Her description has as its embedded structure the notion of evolution from low to high, from savage to civilized, and at the apex of this evolution are what Eichler terms "Aryan" elements. Her work mirrors the same model of evolutionary progress portrayed in the ethnological exhibits of world's fairs.

Eichler's *Customs* is about a commonplace concern, etiquette, yet present within it is the ideology that places the white race at the apex of all that is refined. This is in keeping with an assortment of products put forth during the first quarter of the twentieth century that consistently, whether consciously or through default, reiterated the believed superiority of whiteness.

•

World's fairs, settlement houses, public schools, and etiquette books are four examples of vehicles that in the first quarter of the twentieth century sustained conceptions of white superiority and whiteness as the normative American identity. They were joined by many more, of course: newspapers, literature, museums, movies, and even street life. The millions who partook of these cultural avenues were treated to a constant flow of images that expunged the racial variety that was part of American reality. Placed in its stead was a cultural pantheon enshrining the desirability of whiteness. The autobiographies of those with white skin who came from many nations to this one afford an outsider's view of this pantheon and how cultural agents within it transformed that view to an insider's vision in which whiteness became a privileged social category. These narratives reveal whiteness to be more an idea than a skin color, an idea formulated through spectacle, myth, and enforced conformity. In an essentially romantic genre detailing the rise from "alien" adversity to American prosperity, these stories of migrants seeking new places reveal the monoracializing of American identity and how this was accomplished through means so obvious and pervasive they were essentially invisible.

5

Naming the Nameless
for the Greater Good

> Difference and dialogue are impossible here.
> —*Eric Cheyfitz*

MICHEL FOUCAULT did not invent theory; Jacques Derrida did not invent theory; the barbers in my son's barbershop did. As they fade, edge, and trim, they discourse upon histories, nations, civilizations, and all manner of human thought and invention. One "text" they are particularly fond of deconstructing is The White Man. After one session in which they examined this construct from a psychoanalytic, a Marxist, a Hegelian, and a poststructuralist perspective, one barber concluded by saying, I wanna meet this white man y'all keep talkin' 'bout. He of course never will, because this white man is essentially a fabrication. In hearing these barbers speak, however, the power of this fabrication materially to affect the lives of many becomes evident. Also evident are the compelling reasons why the ideology which created it must be dissected.

In studies of history, culture, and theory, the "why" of the study often gets lost. In reflecting upon whiteness, something that exists everywhere and nowhere in American culture, there is an even greater danger of losing sight of the "why." As veiled as it may sometimes be, however, an awareness of whiteness as an ideology, a system of traditions practices and beliefs that privileges some over the many, is vital to the continued thriving of a multiracial, multiethnic, and multireligious culture. Failure to question the impact of this ideology makes a nation of many peoples and traditions vulnerable to increased divisiveness.

The continued privileging of whiteness ultimately benefits no one. It fosters in those who can claim its privileges a distancing from those they perceive as being not like them; and it fosters in those who cannot claim its privileges a defensive anger as they tire of its arbitrary standards being used as the measure of their worth. To sustain an ideology of whiteness is to sanction the violent acts of persons who may be equally marginalized as those they victimize and to nourish a growing enmity toward those perceived as enjoying its advantages. The ideology that fuels whiteness strips us of our individuality and makes us formulaic representations of what we imagine one another to be.

Our literature reveals to us that the system of beliefs and values that hiearchized race and placed whiteness at the apex solved a number of problems for the propertied English settlers, who sought to consolidate and maintain their identities as well as their economic and social power. It helped them categorize inhabitants of a world unfamiliar to them and thereby justify increasing land encroachment. It helped justify the denial of basic human rights to peoples brought to the United States and enslaved as unpaid laborers. It helped solidify a populace at a time when factionalism and political dissension among many white ethnicities and classes threatened the establishment of a fledgling republic. The ideology of whiteness wove together arbitrary traits of hair color, eye color, skin color, religious belief, language, morality, and class into a network of standards against which those it defined as different could be measured. It cemented a code of authority that haunts even contemporary questions of national self-definition and equal access.

Conceptions of whiteness assisted in forging ties among people who had no natural ties, by inventing a series of myths to hold them together. Loosely strung historical events were made to tell the story of how propertied, white, English settlers sought to practice their religion freely and came to America with the blessing of "the one and only God"; how they conquered a sometimes unforgiving landscape and built a promised land that would subsequently incorporate many "huddled masses." This mytho-history fostered a sense that this group and its descendants were the sole agents responsible for creating this new state and were thus the rightful heirs to its liberties, which only they could grant or deny to others. From these mythologies emerged a constellation of rhetoric and rights in which words painted an idealistic vision of equal access yet policy narrowly limited that access to a few.

Over the course of its existence in the United States, American mytho-history became an ideology that gave whiteness prominence but also deracialized and universalized it. It named the laws that assisted its growth, the images that perpetuated its values, simply as "American" creations. The 1862 Homestead Act is an example. Though cast as a means of expanding the nation's frontier through government granting of "free" land (or perhaps a more accurate characterization would be land formerly inhabited by Native Americans) to white working-class laborers, the act became a means of perpetuating race privilege when African Americans were barred from land ownership under its provisions.[1] The same can be said for the right to vote, the right to run for public office, and the right to serve on juries.[2] Cultural representations functioned similarly. Canonized American literature and art preponderantly cast universal human qualities, such as the capacity for romantic love, love of family, social and personal responsibility, and the desire for freedom, as racial traits that characterized white American character, while denying the existence of these qualities in nonwhite races and placing in their stead barbarism, servility, savageness, and ignorance. This appropriation of the universal assisted in making the ideological nature of whiteness less discernible. By ascribing common qualities to a select racial group, the ideology of whiteness could accomplish exclusion without explicit rationales of racial superiority; instead, it could point to "intrinsic" human inadequacies as endemic to nonwhites and use these as rationales for racial privileging.

The ideology of whiteness taught that there was a single group of people who accomplished anything that was worth accomplishing in the United States, and that they did it alone.

It consequently appropriated the inventions of other groups to sustain this fallacy. The automatic traffic light, refrigeration units for trucks, and automatic air brakes are among many African American inventions that were expropriated by industrial giants such as General Electric and Bell Telephone and termed "American" industrial ingenuity.[3] The tales of Brer Rabbit were based on African folktales, but were lifted by writers such as Joel Chandler Harris and termed "quaint," local-color tales of the plantation tradition. It has been suggested that even the voice of that all-American white boy Huck Finn derives from the talk of a "bright, simple, guileless little darkey boy," Sociable Jimmy.[4] Appropriation of the inventions of a multiracial nation to the cause of advantaging one race is one of the ironies that characterized this ideology. Often the very qualities and products whiteness used to assert racial superiority originated among the groups it sought to demean.

While the ideology that privileges white skin served many in the past, today it is problematic, for it limits its beneficiaries to an increasingly nescient and narrow sphere. Sequestered in a cloistered space that by degrees grows increasingly stifling, many are often unaware of its constraining nature. This ideology encourages them to live in their diverse world handicapped by an ignorance of the other cultures, traditions, and perspectives that constitute the majority of their world. It limits awareness of their *own* culture and their *own* history because it defines elements of both as Native American or Latina (o) or Asian American or African American and assesses these as not worthy of study, not worth knowing, because they are "marginal" histories. It encourages them to fear contact with or feel a subtle, indefinable discomfort when in the presence of others not like them. Each encounter with someone from a different racial classification potentially necessitates a response to alleviate this discomfort. Such responses can range from the seemingly innocuous "I never see you as _____, I just see you as a person," which marks a person's difference as something not human, to the more pernicious demonizing of difference that creates stereotypic apparitions—drug lords, welfare queens, terrorists, muggers, foreign competitors—to rationalize feelings of discomfort.

Ultimately, the insularity that whiteness needs to maintain itself—the self-absorbed conversations, the moving only within a set of like people, the exclusive living enclaves—will become difficult to maintain. As demographics shift and the race of the traditional majority in the United States becomes just one more minority, as the racial and cultural make-up of huge areas in the United States metamorphose, contestations to whiteness's privilege will persist, and increasing resources will have to be devoted to rationalizing its preeminence. As it struggles to adjust to this new demographic landscape, an ideology of whiteness no doubt will continue to conjure imagined scapegoats as justifications for enacting policies for its own conservation, but it will do so not in specifically racial terms, however, but rather in new rhetoric that minimizes the risk of alienating outright an increasingly diverse population. "Personal responsibility" will absolve whites who have access to the greatest portion of the nation's resources from considering public policy that would bring about a more equitable distribution of these resources; "the quest for a better quality of life" will justify the separatism that results from "white flight" from areas with substantial racially mixed populations;[5] and "security at home and abroad" will justify militaristic initiatives to protect the interests of a dominant white group and immigration initiatives that turn American borders into American barriers.

What the ideology of whiteness provides to those who affirm it is a perceived safety from contestation. Not all who are generally classified white are comfortable with this safety zone, but nonetheless they benefit from it. In a probing, self-reflective essay, scholar Peggy McIntosh characterizes this passive benefit when she describes how she has come to understand the privilege that derives from being classified as white:

> I have come to see white privilege as an invisible package of unearned assets that I can count on cashing in each day, but about which I was "meant" to remain oblivious. White privilege is like an invisible weightless knapsack of special provisions, assurances, tools, maps, guides, codebooks, passports, visas, clothes, compass, emergency gear, and blank checks. (71).

A key observation that helps to shed light on the nature of white privilege is McInstosh's reference to the design by which she is "meant" to remain oblivious to the advantages whiteness accords. The ideology that empowers it effects this obliviousness by identifying perquisites as the results of self-reliance or moral character or as the benefits of being an American.

McIntosh goes on to list forty-six privileges that she did not recognize as such; among them,

7. When I am told about our national heritage or about "civilization," I am shown that people of my color made it what it is. . . .

12. I can go into a book shop and count on finding the writing of my race represented, into a supermarket and find the staple foods that fit with my cultural traditions, into a hairdresser's shop and find someone who can deal with my hair.

13. Whether I use checks, credit cards, or cash, I can count on my skin color not to work against the appearance that I am financially reliable. . . .

15. I did not have to educate our children to be aware of systemic racism for their own daily physical protection. . . .

18. I can swear, or dress in secondhand clothes, or not answer letters, without having people attribute these choices to the bad morals, the poverty, or the illiteracy of my race. . . .

22. I can remain oblivious to the language and customs of persons of color who constitute the world's majority without feeling in my culture any penalty for such oblivion. (73–74)

The advantages McIntosh identifies would probably not be realized as perquisites by those enjoying them; yet they become so because some within a culture can enjoy them and others cannot. They are so intrinsic to how American culture responds to this classification that they are never recognized as the assets of a privileged race. Yet their unquestioned existence and their beneficence even to those who vehemently oppose inequitable race privilege amount to a continuing validation of the ideology sustaining them.

The ideology of whiteness is an anachronistic hierarchy that no longer contributes to the general good. Its history began in contention and repression, and those qualities still inform its existence today. Based on myth, it still permits some to presume, knowingly or unknowingly, an unearned superiority to those who are different from them. The social hazards that stem from a belief in this ideology are outlined by Richard Slotkin as he describes the consequences of not separating cultural myth from cultural reality:

> A people unaware of its myths is likely to continue living by them, though the world around that people may change and demand changes in their psychology, their world view, their ethics, and their institutions. . . .
>
> The voluminous reports of presidential commissions on violence, racism, and civil disorder have recently begun to say to us what artists like Melville and Faulkner had earlier prophesied: that myths reach out of the past to cripple, incapacitate, or strike down the living. (4–5)

Contestations over affirmative action, immigration laws, reproductive rights, multiculturalism in education; the increasing isolation of segments of American culture from the larger culture; the self-hatred engendered in many who do not fit a narrow set of physical ideals; and "white flight" from increasingly multiracial and multiethnic areas are all examples of the crippling effects of clinging to a myth that has no meaning in modern America. Giving further credence to Slotkin's point, another commission on race recently has been formed, this one convened by President Bill Clinton in August 1997, chaired by historian John Hope Franklin, and envisioned as a "conversation on race." Perhaps the reason this conversation and many like it seem recurrent events in American life is that the root cause of the inequity they seek to address has not changed. Much of our dialogue on race has concerned itself with making an existing system, founded on a belief in the supremacy of whiteness, more amenable to the concerns of a diverse population, and not with changing that system. From this perspective, any move toward greater racial parity is doomed to be seen as liberal white largesse, pandering to special interests, or engaging in identity politics. Against the presumption that white Americans are the only Americans to have shaped the history of the United States, designing more accurate school curricula will always seem to be catering to "political correctness" as opposed to creating a more responsible historical record. Against a backdrop that stresses conforming to the cultural standards of white Americans, multilingual education will always be seen as special treatment and not as a means of cohering diverse linguistic communities. As long as the producers of popular media continue to presume that nonwhites' experience is too alien to "sell," token representations against the backdrop of a white norm will persist in movies, television, and advertisements. As long as white Americans are implicitly deemed more deserving of the resources of the United States than other groups, affirmative action goals that seek to counter unnamed white privilege and achieve social justice will be seen as preferential treatment. While the psychic wage of whiteness compensates for the disproportionate distribution of the country's greatest share of its social and economic resources to the smallest segment of its population, eradicating poverty, illiteracy, and affliction will not be realizable national goals.

The ideology of whiteness encourages attitudes that can only deepen cultural stratification. Its principles of exclusion construct difference, the very characteristic that will come to symbolize the United States in the next century, as something negative, something to be feared. It continues to use the chimera of race to make impossible a vision of connectedness that exists within and across cultures. It encourages identification with a particular group in the interest not of celebrating traditions but of maintaining bulwarks amid a perceived rising tide of difference. The ideology that has created a race and allowed it to exist in a space of social privilege, will keep a nation on the verge of a remarkable cultural experiment from asking the right questions and following the correct course to realizing its full potential.

Notes

Notes to Chapter 1

1. It is primarily in the 1980s and 1990s that studies specifically interrogating whiteness, independent of general discussions of theories of race formation, have emerged. See Hill; Haney-López; Frankenberg; Allen; Morrison, *Playing in the Dark*; Roediger; and Saxton. In addition, organizations such as the American Studies Association and the Modern Language Association have sponsored sessions on whiteness at their annual conferences.

2. The aim of my phrasing here is to employ a terminology that shifts whiteness from a position of centrality and encourages reflection on the manner in which naming race categories recapitulates the notion that white is a norm against which other races are to be measured.

3. The debate as to whether race is a sociological or biological category is an extensive and ongoing one. To avoid repetition, this study does not take up this issue but refers readers to other, more exhaustive analyses. See Omi and Winant; Appiah, "The Conservation of 'Race'"; Sollors; Allen; Hudson; Dominguez; and F. James Davis.

4. One means of maintaining the distinction between white-skinned whites and white-skinned nonwhites was the "one-drop rule." Formed during the era of slavery and cemented during the Jim Crow era, this "rule" defined anyone having African ancestry, however remote or difficult to document, as "black." The "one-drop rule" was distinctly North American. In other cultures, being white was conceived of more as a social status. Theodore Allen makes reference to colonial Hispanic America, in which it was possible to purchase a "royal certificate of whiteness" regardless of one's race. See Allen, 27. For extensive discussions of the "one-drop rule" and its influence in defining who was white and who was black, see F. James Davis and Dominguez.

5. Bernard Mandel and Edmund Morgan offer informative studies of white laborers who were aware of how race and class were intertwined systems of oppression. See Mandel; Morgan, *American Slavery*. One of the most enduring and enlightening studies of the manipulation of race in class construction is W. E. B. Du Bois's *Black Reconstruction*.

6. Of the designation *Franj*, Maalouf writes, "[C]ontemporary Arab historians and chroniclers ... spoke not of Crusades, but of Frankish wars, or 'the Frankish invasions'. The word designating the Franks was transcribed in many ways, according to region, author, and period. In the various chronicles, we find Faranj, Faranjat, Ifrang, Ifranjat, and other variants. For the sake of consistency, I have chosen to use the briefest form, *Franj*, a word which is used in colloquial Arabic even today to designate Westerners, and the French in particular" (foreword).

7. I have handily glossed over approximately two hundred years of history. In *White over Black*, Winthrop Jordan gives a detailed analysis of changing racial attitudes during this period, paying particular

attention to English attitudes toward race and the subsequent influence these had on attitudes in the United States.

8. In addition to justifying an economic enterprise, one of the aims of this document was to assure English skeptics that the Virginia Company's establishment of a colony in the Americas would not lead to the excess of cruelty to Native Americans that was associated with Spanish colonization and chronicled by Bartolomé de Las Casas, Catholic priest and bishop of Chiapas. See Hanke.

9. For further figures and documentation, see Bailyn.

10. An instance such as this reveals what Toni Morrison and other cultural critics have cited as the manner in which white identity and status are formed and privileged against the presence and status of African Americans. In other cases the Scottish were not so fortunate, however. For a history of Scottish enslavement, see Chambers. For additional discussions of how the terms *white* and *free*, on the one hand, and how *black* and *perpetual slave*, on the other, became synonymous, see Jordan, Allen, Roediger, Saxton.

11. For a discussion of the challenges facing indentured servants in the United States during the eighteenth century, see Bailyn.

12. Allen notes that the plantation of Ulster, organized two years after Jamestown in 1609, was envisioned as akin to plantations being established in the United States; see 115, 272 n. 5.

13. Other scholars caution not to read this split too simplistically. See Siebert, 537.

14. Of the veracity of Byrd's descriptions, the editor of the *Histories*, William K. Boyd, comments, "As a description of the frontier region along the Virginia-Carolina border its general tone is true to nature; but certain details leave on the mind of the reader misconceptions regarding conditions and policies in North Carolina" (xxiii).

15. Boyd's note defines quern stones as "Stones for querns, or hand mills" (304).

16. In chapter 5 of his work, Gossett provides a thorough discussion of the impact of Teutonic origins theory on American conceptions of the state and national identity.

17. For more information on the relationship between racial conceptions and manifest destiny, see Horsman.

18. When the fascination with Anglo-Saxon heritage began to wane in the early twentieth century, advocates of scientific racism such as self-declared "scientific humanist" Theodore Lothrop Stoddard favored the use of the term *Nordic*, characterizing the descendants from this racial "tribe" in the following manner: "[T]here seems to be no question that the Nordic is far and away the most valuable type; standing, indeed, at the head of the whole human genus" (162).

19. The colonies excluded all women and African American and Native American males from voting and required that white men own property—generally more than forty acres or a house or a farm (with the tools to work it)—to vote. About 40 percent of free white men did not meet this requirement, nearly all of whom were indentured servants. A smaller portion were unmarried or newly married males. In the late 1700s, many states eradicated property ownership as a prerequisite for voting, and by the 1800s, most states entering the Union constitutionally provided for universal white male suffrage. See Wells, Dinkin.

Notes to Chapter 2

1. The primary focus of this chapter is an investigation of documents that are generally considered to constitute the earliest *literature* of the United States. Other studies trace the formation of whiteness

through laws, statutes, public policy, and practice. See Allen and Haney-López.

2. Some critics read Smith as both a travel writer and a writer of myths heavily influenced by the medieval traditions. See Rozwenc and Cheyfitz.

3. Smith's were not the only writings to lay the foundation for English colonialism in North America. Where Smith employed travel narrative to accustom English minds to the notion that the New World was theirs, others employed the rhetoric of religious destiny. In *A True Discourse of the Present Estate of Virginia* (1615), Ralphe Hamor employed religious right to justify imperialist enterprise. Designed to rationalize the Virginia venture to a country of origin that was growing increasingly skeptical of its feasibility, Hamor's text makes use of seventeenth-century Calvinist rhetoric. The settlers were not mercenaries, solely engaged in an economic enterprise; they were pilgrims following God's will in seeking to convert and redeem a "heathen" people: "*[F]or what is more excellent, more precious and more glorious, then to convert a heathen Nation from worshipping the divell, to the saving knowledge, and true worship of God in Christ Jesus? what more praiseworthy and charitable, then to bring a* sauage *people from barbarisme unto civillitie? what more honourable unto our countrey, then to reduce a farre disioyned forraigne nation, under the due obedience of our dread* Soveraigne the Kings Majestie? *what more convenient then to have good seates abroade for our over flowing multitudes of people at home? what more profitable then to purchase great wealth, which most now adaies gape after overgreedily? All which benefits are assuredly to bee had and obtained, by well and plentifully upholding of the plantation in* Virginia" (48). Hamor's religious imperative quickly becomes an economic one by the end of this passage, as the conversion of a "heathen Nation" gives way to the acquisition of "great wealth" that settlement of Virginia promises.

By fusing mercantilist expansion with the rhetoric of religious mission, his text sanctions as divine destiny English land acquisition in America, casting it as a seventeenth-century religious crusade. English desire to migrate to the New World was thus rationalized as a means of spreading God's work, and English determination to remain despite hardship was portrayed as obeying God's will.

4. The emphasis on the New England record here should not imply that no such vision manifested itself in Virginia. Perry Miller, in *Errand into the Wilderness*, was one of the earliest scholars to argue that in addition to detailing the challenges faced by the Virginia Company in its attempt to maintain a colony, the writings produced in Virginia share many of the religious imperatives produced in New England. See chap. 4.

5. In *Worlds of Wonder*, David Hall cautions against the sweeping use of the term *Puritan* to encompass what in actuality is a collection of many varied reform sects; see 8–9.

Defined succinctly by Robert Daly, the Puritans' covenant held "that God works through history to assure the triumph of His people and the overthrow of their enemies." Based on "the Deuteronomic Formula, [it] implies a sense of special destiny. . . . Early Christians transferred the sense of special destiny from the Jews to themselves and took the promise of divine assistance quite literally. They insisted that earthly events gave evidence for the truth of their religion" (558). Perry Miller offers a thorough discussion of how the Puritans adapted the belief in covenant to meet secular challenges by creating, at different stages in their history, a covenant of grace, a social covenant, a church covenant, and a federal covenant; see *The New England Mind*, chap. 13–16.

6. My emphasis on the Puritans is not to suggest theirs was the only vision of New England society. In *New English Canaan*, Thomas

Morton gives a portrait of the more secular elements of New England and their contentions with the religious magistrates. The Puritans do, however, exert a strong influence on the written record of the American imagination. Richard Slotkin, in discussing colonial accounts of wars with Native Americans, notes the impact of Puritan vision on the early American creative imagination: "It was within this genre of colonial Puritan writing that the first American mythology took shape—a mythology in which the hero was the captive or victim of devilish American savages and in which his (or her) heroic quest was for religious conversion and salvation" (21). For works treating the influence of Puritan philosophy on the culture of the United States, see Bercovitch, *Puritan Origins of the American Self*, and Miller, *New England Mind*.

7. Difference was not only represented in writing; it became actively reinforced through legal means. Statutes designed to regulate the interaction between the English and peoples of Native American and African descent exhibit a growing separatist stance. A 1606 Virginia statute demonstrates both English resolve for permanent settlement and English willingness to coexist with Native Americans: "[A]nd wee doe hereby determine and ordaine, that every person and persons being our subjects of every the said collonies and plantations shall from time to time well entreate those salvages in those parts, and use all good meanes to draw the salvages and heathen people . . . of the territories and countries adjoining to the true service and knowledge of God, and that all just, kind and charitable courses, shall be holden with such of them as shall conforme themselves to any good and sociable traffique and dealing with the subjects of us, our heires and successors, which shall be planted there" (Hening, 1:74). This tolerance is clearly diminished in Virginia statues recorded in 1629 and 1631: "It *is ordered* that every commander of the severall plantations . . . shall have power and authoritie to levy a partie of men out

of the inhabitants of that place . . . and to imploy those men against the Indians, when they shall assault us neere unto our habitations, or when they in their discretion shall deeme it convenient to cleare the woods and the parts neere adioyning when the Indians shall bee a hunting or when they have any certaine knowledge of the Indian's aboad in those places" (1629); "*It is also ordered*, That the warr begun uppon the Indians bee effectually followed, and that noe peace bee concluded with them. And likewise that all marches which shall hereafter bee ordered and appoynted against them, be prosecuted and followed with all dilligence" (1629); "It *is ordered*, That no person or persons shall dare to speake or parlie with any Indians either in the woods or in any plantation, yf he can possibly avoyd it" (1631) (Hening, 1:140, 153, 167). A similar statute regulates the interaction of English and African Americans. In a 1630 Virginia decree, Hugh Davis is "to be soundly whipped, before an assembly of Negroes and others for abusing himself to the dishonor of God and shame of Christians, by defiling his body in lying with a negro; which fault he is to acknowledge next Sabbath day" (Hening, 1:146). Here Davis's offense is cast as an offense against God and Christianity, and public punishment, meant to dissuade both races from crossing racial boundaries, is the censure.

8. It is interesting to consider how this description compares to later descriptions Bradford gave of Native Americans. Just as the Puritans would express a fear of the North American wilderness's effect on their community, so here Bradford worried about the more urbane Dutch "wilderness" his people were exposed to and about the potential loss of cultural identity: "[O]f all sorrows most heavy to be borne, was that many of their children, by these occasions and the great licentiousness of youth in that country, and the manifold temptations of the place, were drawn away by evil examples into extravagant and

dangerous courses, getting the reins off their necks and departing from their parents. Some became soldiers, others took upon them far voyages by sea, and others some worse courses tending to dissoluteness and the danger of their souls, to the great grief of their parents and dishonour of God. So that they saw their posterity would be in danger to degenerate and be corrupted" (25–26).

9. For further discussion of the ways in which colonial settlers used images of Native Americans as a means to solidify their own group identity, see Slotkin.

10. Bradford was not the only Puritan leader bemoaning increased factionalism. In John Winthrop's description of Massachusetts Bay Colony, the religious contention within this New England community is also evident. In his history the future governor of the Massachusetts Bay Colony wrote, "[E]very occasion increased the contention, and caused great alienation of minds; and the members of Boston (frequenting the lectures of other ministers) did make much disturbance by public questions, and objections to their doctrines, which did any way disagree from their opinions" (Winthrop, 1: 209)

11. Mather's tone contrasts sharply with Bradford's who, in *Of Plymouth Plantation*, related the facts of the same plague. In speaking of going to seek out the land of Massasoit, the chief of the Wampanoag, Bradford stated simply and sympathetically, "They found his place to be forty miles from hence, the soil good and the people not many, being dead and abundantly wasted in the late great mortality, which fell in all these parts about three years before the coming of the English, wherein thousands of them died. They not being able to bury one another, their skulls and bones were found in many places lying still above the ground where their houses and dwellings had been, a very sad spectacle to behold" (97).

12. See John Blassingame, *The Slave Community*, 63.

13. In another passage of the sermon, Mather reflected the closeness between white masters and black slaves through the metaphor of neighbors: "One Table of the *Ten Commandments,* has this for the Sum of it; *Thou shalt Love thy Neighbour as thy self.* Man, Thy *Negro* is thy *Neighbour*" (5). In a subsequent passage Mather noted, "They are more nearly *Related* unto us, than many others are; we are more fully *capable* to do for them, than for many others" (6). On a literal level, both passages indicate how African slaves and European masters lived together in close quarters; but on a more figurative level, both, especially the latter, might be said to represent the way in which constructions of whiteness need blackness to give them meaning.

14. For thorough discussions of the print distribution network that made oral sermons available to many in printed form, see David Hall, chap. 1, and Davidson, chap. 2 and 4.

15. For an account of the number of colonists taken into captivity from the later seventeenth to the mid-eighteenth century, see Coleman.

16. The captivity narratives also share many similarities with the travel narratives and visionary documents. Many of the captives, in telling their tales, naturalized readers to the New World by introducing them to native practices, fauna, rituals, and language. In addition, in many of the narratives are reiterations of the principles of Puritan theology, particularly the notion of covenant. John Gyles and Mary Rowlandson provide two examples. In his 1736 narrative Gyles, who was captured at age ten and spent six years among the Abenaki, includes *Two Indian Fables* and provided early ethnography under headings such as *Of The Beaver, Of the Hedgehog or Urchin, Of Their Feasting before They Go out to War*, and *Of Their Mourning for the Dead, and Feast After It* (Vaughan and Clark, 115–20). Through its blending of expressive forms the structure of his narrative illustrates cul-

tural fusion, as when Gyles inserts allusions to sources as varied as *Europa's Rape* and the *Art of Cookery* into passages containing indigenous American themes. Also an indication of the ancestry of the narrative is the captive's employment of the ideology of covenant. The title of the second and earliest surviving edition of Mary Rowlandson's narrative was *The Soveraignity and Goodness of God, Together, with the Faithfulness of His Promises Displayed; Being a Narrative of the Captivity and Restoration of Mrs. Mary Rowlandson*, and throughout, every event is read as a means of reaffirming the truth of her religion. Visible in Rowlandson's narrative as well, however, are the strains placed upon the covenant by greater exposure to a diverse populace. In "The Twentieth Remove," for example, she catalogs God's providences made evident to her throughout her captivity, but the presence of another race complicates her interpretation: "I can but stand in admiration to see the wonderful power of God, in providing for such a vast number of our enemies in the wilderness where there was nothing to be seen, but from hand to mouth. . . . It is said, Psalm 81:13, 14, 'Oh that my people had hearkened to me, and Israel had walked in my wayes, I should soon have subdued their enemies, and turned my hand against their adversaries.' But now our perverse and evil carriages in the sight of the Lord have so offended Him, that instead of turning His hand against them, the Lord feeds & nourishes them up to be a scourge to the whole land" (51–52). Rowlandson can read God's beneficence to all humans only as a condemnation of Puritan lapses. Only by casting the thriving of another race as God's wrath against Puritan declension can her belief in the covenantal relationship be sustained.

17. Cotton Mather's "A Brand Pluck'd Out of the Burning" provides evidence of the imaginative fusion of blackness and the devil with the ultimate aim of demonizing Native Americans. Describing a

vision experienced by a young woman who was thought to be possessed, Mather wrote, "There exhibited himself unto her a Divel having the Figure of A Short and a Black Man; . . . hee was not of a Negro, but of a Tawney, or an Indian colour . . . with strait Hair" (in Burr, 261).

18. Incidents recalling loss of self-mastery are plentiful in the narratives; see Quentin Stockwell (Vaughan and Clark, 89) and Elizabeth Hanson (Vaughan and Clark, 235). The narratives also exhibit ample concern of slippage into alien culture; see John Williams (Vaughan and Clark, 225).

19. One captivity narrative by a woman reverses this image of the passive female, however. In her 1697 tale, Hannah Dustan relates wreaking vengeance on her captors and receiving notoriety and awards. Vaughan and Clark note, "Despite the brevity of her story, Hannah Dustan's is among the most famous. Her bold and bloody escape earned her legendary honors in New England's annals and, more recently, a place in *Notable American Women* (Cambridge, Mass., 1971), where she is listed among the 'heroines.' And as Cotton Mather noted at the end of his version of her captivity, she and her companions gained material honors too: a L50 reward from the Massachusetts government and a 'very generous token of his favor' from Governor Francis Nicholson of Maryland" (161). I suggest, however, that Dustan's narrative likely was so celebrated not because it portrayed a woman liberating herself and debunking the myth of feminine helplessness but because its scene of retribution is a rare one in captivity narratives, and one in which readers who saw themselves as victims could experience a vicarious vindication.

20. For arguments that white female authors often depicted an identification between white women and racially marginalized peoples, see Baym.

21. For studies surveying sexual constructions of the white female, see Welter, duCille.

22. Vaughan and Clark note that popular representations of the sexual threat northeastern Native American men ostensibly posed to white female captives were the products more of imagination than of reality: "[N]o ethnological evidence indicates that northeastern Indians ever raped women prisoners, as Plains Indians sometimes did" (14).

23. The Navigation Acts banned colonial merchants from shipping products such as sugar and tobacco to any place other than England. For further information, see Dickerson. For further discussion of the changes in New England during this time, see Miller, *New England Mind*.

24. For discussions on the social, economic, and political situation of women in the seventeenth and eighteenth centuries, see Koehler, Morgan, and Ulrich.

25. Though universal literacy was by no means the case during the colonial period, the ability to read was widespread enough that publishers believed the printing of sermons and captivity and criminal narratives to be viable economic enterprises. For a more detailed discussion of early American literacy and the dissemination of print media, see Davidson, chap. 1. David D. Hall notes how literate New England society was: "It seems likely that most people in New England learned to read as children. Of no less importance is the fact that everyone had access to the Bible in his native language, and to cheap books marketed especially for lay readers. Always there were some who did not own a Bible or lacked fluency in reading. But we can safely assume that most of the emigrants to New England had broken through into the world of print" (7).

Notes to Chapter 3

1. Many of these representations or their variations can be found in works as varied as Harriet Beecher Stowe's *Uncle Tom's Cabin*, Edward S. Ellis's *Seth Jones*, and Owen Wister's *The Virginian*. For fuller discussions of the variety of types present throughout American literature from the colonial period to the late nineteenth century, see Slotkin, Fiedler, and Davidson.

2. For a thorough discussion of the Victorian ideals of femininity and how they influenced American constructions of women in the nineteenth century, see Welter.

3. For further analyses of these contestations in American culture, see Dinnerstein, Nichols, and Reimers; McWilliams; and Takaki.

4. A sampling of the different lights shed on *Moby-Dick* can be garnered from the following studies: Lawrance Thompson's *Melville's Quarrel with God*; Harry Levin's *The Power of Blackness*; Nathalia Wright's *Melville's Use of the Bible*; H. Bruce Franklin's *The Wake of the Gods*; and Henry F. Pommer's *Milton and Melville*. In their annotated edition of *Moby-Dick*, Harrison Hayford, Herschel Parker, and G. Thomas Tanselle identify the many influences at work in the novel: "[W]e report in this paragraph some of what the best authorities have concluded about literary influences on *Moby-Dick*. It was pervasively influenced by the Bible (in particular the Book of Job . . . the Book of Jonah. . . .) by Shakespeare's plays . . . by Milton's *Paradise Lost* . . . by Marlowe's *Dr. Faustus* and Goethe's *Faust* . . . by Robert Burton, whose *Anatomy of Melancholy* served as this pondering-man's textbook on morbid psychology; by Sir Thomas Browne . . . by Thomas Hope's *Anastasius; or, Memoirs of a Greek* . . . by Mary Shelley's *Frankenstein* . . . by Dante . . . by Pierre Bayle's dictionary and Montaigne's essays . . . by Coleridge's lecture on *Hamlet* . . . by Car-

lyle . . . by Sterne's *Tristram Shandy* . . . by De Quincey's *Confessions*" (Melville, 646–47).

5. In their extensive appendix to *Moby-Dick*, Hayford, Parker, and Tanselle offer an explanation for why the title of the novel is hyphenated yet the name of the whale is not. I have chosen to follow their practice and hyphenate the novel's title but not the whale's name. See Melville, 810–12.

6. The source of the novel's duality is partially suggested in a letter Melville wrote to his friend and reader Nathaniel Hawthorne: "What I feel most moved to write, that is banned,—it will not pay. Yet, altogether, write the *other* way I cannot" (Davis and Gilman, eds., *Letters of Melville*, 128). Here Melville expressed his conflict between being a writer who desired to create a popular and salable work and one who wished to write a novel with a deeper and more complex meaning. He resolved this duality by writing to satisfy both needs. As Hayford, Parker, and Tanselle note in the appendix to their edition of *Moby-Dick*, "[A] penetrating reader could have detected, pervading the romantic adventures . . . a certain independent disposition to find things wrong with the established order of society; to question and rebel against constituted authority" (Melville, 592).

7. See Stone, 349–50.

8. Some critics read Melville's subversion of whiteness with a skeptical eye. Edward Stone notes, "It is true that to Ahab, Moby-Dick is the incarnation of evil, and Moby-Dick is the *white* whale; that the most appalling aspect of Creation that the *Pequod* encounters is the great *white* squid,—that 'unearthly, formless, chance-like apparition,' that omen of disaster that the brave Starbuck addresses fearfully as 'thou white ghost!' . . . It is also true that, to Ishmael's mind, all men at all times have shared this instinctive revulsion against whiteness in some forms, so that the dread may be called universal. But the

horror in these instances is actually a limited one. Balancing it are the numerous universal associations that Ishmael makes, in 'The Whiteness of the Whale,' between this color and the good, the pure, even the celestial" (349–50).

9. For complete annotations of the references in "Extracts," see Hayford, Parker, and Tanselle, in Melville.

10. See Linnaeus. For ways in which Linnaeus's theories fueled racial debates of the eighteenth and nineteenth centuries, see Jordan, Gossett.

11. For specific applications of phrenology to race theories, and for a general discussion of phrenology in the nineteenth-century United States, see Davies and Arthur Wrobel.

12. Frank's discussion of the art mentioned in *Moby-Dick* is elaborate and engaging. He notes that the artworks alluded to in the novel are central to its composition: "Yet in all . . . Mellvilliana accumulated over the past three generations, one region of *Moby-Dick* remains virtually unexplored. The illustrations and pictures, especially the ones mentioned specifically or alluded to generically in three middle chapters, have attracted only general interpretive notice and minimal pictorial attention. More often, the entire sequence of 'pictorial' chapters has been passed over as tangential to the narrative. While the Whaling Bard is touted as perhaps America's greatest master of epic prose, exploration of his pictorial eye, the 'fearful symmetry' of his visual sensibilities, has never been properly or comprehensively connected with the pictures that he himself cites, nor with the types and prototypes generally familiar to his generation. These are Melville's sources as surely as his reading" (xv).

13. What is important to note about these visual representations is how they reflect and respond to the political, social, and economic need of the dominant culture that created them. See Slotkin for a

detailed analysis of transformations in the representations of Native Americans—how, for example, their characterization as fearsome savages, raping white Englishwomen and killing children, assisted in justifying their extermination during the colonial times. Once removals were complete, the representation evolved into nostalgic portraits of Native American figures against naturalistic backdrops of waterfalls or plains, soothing to an increasingly mechanized and socially complex culture that longed for pristine wilderness and past social innocence. For a similar examination of shifting representations of African Americans, see the film *Ethnic Notions* (California News Reel, 1986), which investigates how, for example, their portrayal as childlike, happy "darkies" who needed slavery's protection and structure justified the "peculiar institution." After slavery was ended, these portraits were replaced by postbellum depictions of "coons" who, without the control of slavery, reverted to barbarism and were therefore not fit to be fully enfranchised American citizens.

14. See Fiedler, 370–88. Another critic to treat Melville's homoeroticism is Georges Sarotte; see *Like a Brother, Like a Lover*.

15. For a thorough discussion of the theme of the frontier in American literature and its relation to racial constructions, see Slotkin.

Notes to Chapter 4

1. Horace Bridges might be taken as an exception to this pattern at first glance. Yet even his identification of cultural pluralism as a key element of American identity is vague in its naming of race; instead, he refers to diverse "nationalities" and "culture types": "The value of the American experiment would be lost if this nation became conformed exclusively to the type of any one of the nationalities which have entered into its composition. The business of America is to pro-

duce a new type of national character and civilization, by the cross-fertilization of the many culture-types which the Republic has absorbed and is absorbing" (40). Though he does not specifically mention race, Bridges does not relegate the American identity to a single type. His vision was rare, however, and more frequent were visions that presumed assimilation to a single ideal.

2. In his autobiography, Jacob Riis also reveals the impact American literature, especially James Fenimore Cooper, had in shaping his conceptions of American identity. Recalling a meeting with Ely Parker (who served as military secretary for General Ulysses S. Grant) and Chief Donehogawa, he writes, "It was not General Parker, however, but Donehogawa, Chief of the Senecas and of the remnant of the once powerful Six Nations, and guardian of the western door of the council lodge, that appealed to me, who in my boyhood had lived with Leatherstocking and with Uncas and Chingachgook. They had something to do with my coming here, and at last I had for a friend one of their kin" (244).

3. For complete histories of the world's fairs, see Rydell, *All the World's a Fair, World of Fairs*; Badger, Burg.

4. Rydell, *All the World's a Fair*, 4; hereafter cited parenthetically as *ATWF*.

5. The Victorian "cult of domesticity" no doubt influenced these representations of women. According to Daniel Walker Howe, "[T]he most important locus for cultural transmission in Victorian society was the home, and the Victorians acknowledged this with their cult of domesticity. . . . A prominent feature of the Victorian cult of domesticity was the exaltation of motherhood. The high esteem accorded the status of motherhood in Victorian culture was a logical consequence of the importance assigned the mother as an agent of cultural transmission. The mother was an acknowledged

guardian of moral, religious, and other cultural values among American Victorians, and the home was her sphere of influence" (529–530).

6. Racism, it seems, played a part in women's participation in the fair as well. Of the creation of the Woman's Building Rydell writes, "Prominent women in Chicago—led by Bertha Palmer, wife of Chicago hotel magnate Potter Palmer—determined that the World's Columbian Exposition would also include a pavilion dedicated to advancing women's interests. . . . [T]he Board of Lady Managers, consist[ed] of more than one hundred middle- and upper-class women from around the United States. . . . Mirroring the all-white male boards that ran the fair, no African-American women were included on the Board of Lady Managers. The interests of African-American women, in theory, were represented by a white woman from Kentucky. And Native American women were represented by ethnologists from the Smithsonian Institution who organized a display on the ground floor of the Woman's Building entitled 'The Arts of Women in Savagery' " (Carr and Gurney, 52–55).

7. According to Reid Badger, among the most popular sites at the Chicago exposition was the "Brinker's cotton bale exhibit—where miniature cotton bales done up in silk and satin and brass could be purchased as souvenirs from the old ex-slaves who had grown the cotton in 1863" (103).

8. For a fuller history of this movement and its relation to world's fairs, see Rydell, *A World of Fairs*, chap. 2.

9. For a complete biography of Jane Addams, see Allen Davis.

10. Hull-House was willing to address the concerns of African Americans in another part of the city, and with fund-raising help from Jane Addams, a group of settlement workers founded the Wendell Phillips Settlement in an African American district on the West Side

of Chicago. For an article describing the African American experience and Hull-House, see Bowen.

11. In its later years, Hull-House catered to whatever population became part of its environs. During the 1920s the neighborhood became largely Mexican, and gradually African Americans entered as well. These changing demographics caused many tensions, however, among various ethnicities and racial groups. For further information, see Bryan and Davis, 158.

12. A desire to conform ethnic food preparation to a white American norm is evident in Hull-House's attempt to instill good dietary habits. Addams describes her experience in setting up the kitchen at Hull-House: "At that time the New England kitchen was comparatively new in Boston, and Mrs. Richards, who was largely responsible for its foundation, hoped that cheaper cuts of meat and simpler vegetables, if they were subjected to slow and thorough processes of cooking, might be made attractive and their nutritive value secured for the people who so sadly needed more nutritious food. It was felt that this could be best accomplished in public kitchens, where the advantage of scientific training and careful supervision could be secured. One of the residents went to Boston for a training under Mrs. Richards, and when the Hull-House kitchen was fitted under her guidance and direction, our hopes ran high for some modification of the food of the neighborhood. We did not reckon, however, with the wide diversity in nationality and inherited tastes, and while we sold a certain amount of the carefully prepared soups and stews in the neighboring factories . . . and were also patronized by a few households, perhaps the neighborhood estimate was best summed up by the woman who frankly confessed, that the food was certainly nutritious, but that she didn't like to eat what was nutritious, that she liked to eat 'what she'd ruther' " (78).

13. Anne Boylan notes that religious education also contributed to the dissemination of cultural standards: "Education consists of more than learning to read; it encompasses all the means through which a culture transmits its standards and values, including families, newspapers, and churches. From this perspective, the impact of nineteenth-century Sunday schools was dramatic. For through them passed millions of children who came into contact, briefly or for an extended period, with the tenets and world view of evangelical Protestantism. As an agency of cultural transmission, the Sunday school almost rivaled in importance the nineteenth-century public school" (33).

Notes to Chapter 5

1. For further discussion of the Homestead Act and the Free Soil Movement as manifestations of race privilege, see Saxton.

2. For a discussion of the legislative acts that essentially constructed whiteness, see Haney-López and Allen.

3. For information on African American inventors and the appropriation of their innovations, see Brodie, Jenkins.

4. See Fishkin, "From *Was Huck Black?*" 410. In the extended study from which this work is excerpted, *Was Huck Black? Mark Twain and African-American Voices*, Fishkin cites compelling evidence that the model for Huck Finn's voice was a young African American male.

5. Explorations of the latest trend of "white flight" are emerging. See Holmes.

Bibliography

Addams, Jane. *Twenty Years at Hull-House, with Autobiographical Notes.*
1910. Introduction and notes by James Hurt. Urbana: University
of Illinois Press, 1990.

Adorno, T. W., Else Frenkel-Brunswick, Daniel J. Levinson, and R.
Nevitt Sanford. *The Authoritarian Personality.* New York: Harper,
1950.

Allen, Theodore William. *The Invention of the White Race.* Volume 1:
Racial Oppression and Social Control. 2 vols. London: Verso, 1994.

American Historical Association. *The Study of History in Schools: Report
to the American Historical Association.* New York: Macmillan, 1904.

Ames, Nathaniel. *An Astronomical Diary, or, Almanack, For the Year of
our Lord CHRIST, 1769.* New Haven: T. and S. Green, 1769.

Anderson, Benedict. *Imagined Communities: Reflections on the Origin
and Spread of Nationalism.* London: Verso, 1983.

Antin, Mary. *The Promised Land.* Boston: Houghton Mifflin, 1911.

Appiah, Kwame Anthony. "The Conservation of 'Race.' " *Black
American Literature Forum* 23, 1 (1989): 37–60.

———. "The Uncompleted Argument: DuBois and the Illusion of Race." In Gates, 21–37.

Arber, Edward, ed. *The First Three English Books on America*. Birmingham, England: Westminster A. Constable, 1885.

Aristotle. *Politica*. Edited by Benjamin Jowett. New York: Modern Library, 1943.

Arthur. *The Life and Dying Speech of Arthur, a Negro Man, who was Executed at Worcester, October 20th, 1768*. Boston: Kneeland and Adams, 1768.

Badger, Reid. *The Great American Fair: The World's Columbian Exposition and American Culture*. Chicago: Nelson Hall, 1979.

Bailyn, Bernard. *Voyagers to the West: A Passage in the Peopling of America on the Eve of the Revolution*. New York: Knopf, 1987.

Banes, Ruth. "The Exemplary Self: Autobiography in Eighteenth Century America." *Biography* 5 (1982): 226–39.

Baritz, Leon. *City on a Hill: A History of Ideas and Myths in America*. New York: Wiley, 1964.

Barkun, Michael. *Religion and the Racist Right: The Origins of the Christian Identity Movement*. Chapel Hill: University of North Carolina Press, 1994.

Bartels, Emily C. "Imperialist Beginnings: Richard Haklyut and the Construction of Africa." *Criticism* 34 (1992): 517–48.

Baym, Nina. *American Women Writers and the Work of History, 1790–1860*. New Brunswick: Rutgers University Press, 1995.

Bercovitch, Sacvan. *The American Jeremiad*. Madison: University of Wisconsin Press, 1978.

———. *The Puritan Origins of the American Self*. New Haven: Yale University Press, 1975.

Blassingame, John. *The Slave Community*. New York: Oxford University Press, 1979.

Boas, Franz. *The Mind of Primitive Man*. Westport, CT: Greenwoood, 1983.

———. *Race, Language, and Culture*. Chicago: University of Chicago Press, 1982.

Bok, Edward. *The Americanization of Edward Bok: The Autobiography of a Dutch Boy Fifty Years After*. New York: Charles Scribner's Sons, 1920.

Bourdin, H. L., and S. T. Williams. "Crèvecoeur on the Susquehanna 1774–1776." *Yale Review* 14 (1925): 568–80.

Bowen, Louise de Koven. "The Colored People of Chicago." *Survey* (1 November 1913): 117–20. In Bryan and Davis, 133–40.

Boylan, Anne M. *Sunday School: The Formation of an American Institution, 1790–1880*. New Haven: Yale University Press, 1988.

Bradford, Phillips Verner, and Harvey Blume. *Ota Benga: The Pygmy in the Zoo*. New York: St. Martin's, 1992.

Bradford, William. *Of Plymouth Plantation 1620–1647*. New York: Random House, 1981.

Bridges, Horace J. *On Becoming an American, Some Meditations of a Newly Naturalized Immigrant*. Boston: Marshall Jones, 1918.

Brodie, James Michael. *Created Equal: The Lives and Ideas of Black American Innovators*. New York: William Morrow, 1993.

Brooks, Cleanth, R. W. B. Lewis, and Robert Penn Warren, eds. *American Literature: The Makers and the Making*, Book A: *Beginnings to 1826*. New York: St. Martin's, 1973.

Brown, Alexander. *The Genesis of the United States*. 2 vols. Volume 1. New York: Russell and Russell, 1964.

Brumberg, Stephen F. *Going to America, Going to School: The Jewish Immigrant Public School Encounter in Turn-of-the-Century New York City*. New York: Praeger, 1986.

Bryan, Mary Lynn McCree, and Alan Davis. *One Hundred Years at Hull-House*. Bloomington: Indiana University Press, 1990.

Burg, David F. *Chicago's White City of 1893*. Lexington: University Press of Kentucky, 1976.

Burgess, John. *Sovereignty and Liberty*. Volume 1 of *Political Science and Comparative Constitutional Law*. 2 vols. Boston: Ginn and Company, 1890–93.

Burr, George Lincoln, ed. *Narratives of the Witchcraft Cases: 1648–1706*. Original Narratives of Early American History. New York: Charles Scribner's Sons, 1914.

Byrd, William. *William Byrd's Histories of the Dividing Line betwixt Virginia and North Carolina*. Edited by William K. Boyd. New York: Dover Publications, 1967.

Cady, Edwin. *Literature of the Early Republic*. New York: Rinehart, 1950.

Carr, Carolyn Kinder, and George Gurney. *Revisiting the White City: American Art at the 1893 World's Fair*. Washington, DC: Smithsonian Institution, 1993.

Cawelti, John G. "America on Display: The World's Fair of 1876, 1893, 1933." In *The Age of Industrialism in America: Essays in Social Structure and Cultural Values*. Edited by Frederic Cople Jaher, 317–63. New York: Free Press, 1968.

Chambers, Robert. *Domestic Annals of Scotland*. 4 vols. London and Edinburgh, 1861.

Chapman, Charles Edward. *Colonial Hispanic America: A History*. New York: Macmillan, 1933.

Cheng, Lucie, and Edna Bonachich, eds. *Labor Immigration under Capitalism: Asian Workers in the United States before World War II*. Berkeley: University of California Press, 1984.

Cheyfitz, Eric. *The Poetics of Imperialism: Translation and Colonization from the Tempest to Tarzan.* New York: Oxford University Press, 1991.

Church, Benjamin. *Entertaining Passages Relating to Philip's War Which Began in the Month of June, 1675: As also of Expeditions More Lately Made Against the Common Enemy, and Indian Rebels in the Eastern Parts of New England; With some Account of the Divine Providence Towards Benjamin Church, Esquire.* Boston: B. Green, 1716.

Clark, Dennis. "Babes in Bondage: Indentured Irish Children in Philadelphia in the Nineteenth Century." *Pennsylvania Magazine of History and Biography* 101 (1977): 475–86.

Cohen, Daniel. *Pillars of Salt, Monuments of Grace: New England Crime Literature and the Origins of American Popular Culture, 1676–1860.* New York: Oxford University Press, 1993.

Coleman, Emma Lewis. *New England Captives Carried to Canada between 1677 and 1760 during the French and Indian Wars.* 2 vols. Portland, ME: Southworth Press, 1925.

Colony of Connecticut. *The Code of 1650: Being a Compilation of the Earliest Laws and Orders of the General Court of Connecticut; Also the Constitution or Civil Compact, Entered into and Adopted by the Towns of Windsor, Hartford, and Wethersfield in 1638–9; To Which is added, Some Extracts from the Laws and Judicial Proceedings of New Haven Colony, Commonly Called the Blue-Laws.* Hartford: Andrus and Judd, 1836.

Combe, George. *The Constitution of Man.* Hartford: W. Andrus, 1842.

Cooper, James Fenimore. *The Last of the Mohicans.* New York: Penguin, 1986.

Crevecoeur, J. Hector St. John de. *Letters from an American Farmer.* New York: Dolphin-Doubleday, 1963.

Daly, Robert. "William Bradford's Vision of History." *American Literature* 44 (1973): 557–69.

Davidson, Cathy N. *Revolution and the Word: The Rise of the Novel in America*. New York: Oxford University Press, 1986.

Davies, John D. *Phrenology: Fad and Science. A 19th-Century American Crusade*. New Haven: Yale University Press, 1955.

Davis, Allen F. *American Heroine: The Life and Legend of Jane Addams*. New York: Oxford University Press, 1973.

Davis, David Brion. *The Problem of Slavery in the Age of Revolution, 1770–1823*. Ithaca: Cornell University Press, 1975.

Davis, F. James. *Who Is Black? One Nation's Definition*. University Park, PA: Penn State University Press, 1991.

Davis, Merrell R., and William H. Gilman, eds. *The Letters of Herman Melville*. New Haven: Yale University Press, 1960.

Dickerson, Oliver M. *The Navigation Acts and the American Revolution*. Philadelphia: University of Pennsylvania Press, 1951.

Dinkin, Robert J. *Voting in Provincial America: A Study of Elections in the Thirteen Colonies, 1689–1776*. Westport, CT: Greenwood, 1977.

Dinnerstein, Leonard, Roger L. Nichols, and David M. Reimers. *Natives and Strangers: A Multicultural History of Americans*. New York: Oxford University Press, 1996.

Dominguez, Virginia. *White by Definition: Social Classification in Creole Louisiana*. New Brunswick: Rutgers University Press, 1986.

Dosch, Arno. "Our Expensive Cheap Labor." *The World's Work* 26 (1913): 699–703.

Douglass, Mary, and Baron Isherwood. *The World of Goods*. New York: Basic Books, 1979.

DuBois, W. E. B. *Black Reconstruction*. Millwood, NY: Kraus-Thomson Organization, 1976.

———. "The Conservation of Races." In *W. E. B. DuBois Speaks*,

Speeches and Addresses, 1890–1919, Edited by Philip S. Foner, 73–85. New York: Pathfinders, 1970.

———. *Dusk of Dawn: An Essay toward an Autobiography of a Race Concept.* New York: Harcourt Brace, 1940.

———. *The Souls of Black Folk.* New York: Penguin, 1989.

duCille, Ann. *The Coupling Convention: Sex, Text, and Tradition in Black Women's Fiction.* New York: Oxford University Press, 1993.

Duncan, Alexander. *Congressional Globe* 42. 28th Cong. 2d Sess. Washington, D.C., 1845.

Eichler, Lillian (Mrs. Watson). *The Customs of Mankind, with Notes on Modern Etiquette and the Newest Trend in Entertainment.* Garden City, NY: Nelson Doubleday, 1924.

Elliott, Emory. *The Power and the Pulpit in Puritan New England.* Princeton: Princeton University Press, 1975.

Ellis, Edward S. *Seth Jones; or Captives of the Frontier.* In *Seth Jones by Edward Ellis and Deadwood Dick on Deck by Edward L. Wheeler.* Edited by Philip Durham. New York: Odyssey, 1966.

Emerson, Everett, ed. *Major Writers of Early American Literature.* Madison: University of Wisconsin Press, 1972.

Evans, Eli N. *Judah P. Benjamin: The Jewish Confederate.* New York: Free Press, 1988.

Ewen, Elizabeth. *Immigrant Women in the Land of Dollars: Life and Culture on the Lower East Side, 1890–1925.* New York: Monthly Review, 1985.

Fiedler, Leslie. *Love and Death in the American Novel.* New York: Anchor, 1992.

Fishkin, Shelley Fisher. "From *Was Huck Black?*" In *Adventures of Huckleberry Finn. A Case Study in Critical Controversy,* Edited by Gerald Graff and James Phelan. Boston: Bedford Books of St. Martin's, 1995. 407–50.

————. *Was Huck Black? Mark Twain and African-American Voices.* New York: Oxford University Press, 1993.

Fowler, Orson S., and Lorenzo N. Fowler. *Phrenology Proved, Illustrated and Applied.* New York: 1846.

Frank, Stuart. *Herman Melville's Picture Gallery: Sources and Types of the "Pictorial" Chapters of* Moby-Dick. Fairhaven, MA: Edward J. Lefkowicz, 1986.

Frankenberg, Ruth, ed. *Displacing Whiteness: Essays in Social and Cultural Criticism.* Durham: Duke University Press, 1997.

————. *White Women, Race Matters: The Social Construction of Whiteness.* Minneapolis: University of Minnesota Press, 1993.

Franklin, Benjamin. "Conversation on Slavery." *Public Advertiser*, 30 January 1770.

Franklin, H. Bruce. *The Wake of the Gods: Herman Melville's Mythology.* Stanford: Stanford University Press, 1963.

Frost, John. *Pictorial History of the United States of America, from the Discovery by the Northmen in the Tenth Century to the Present Time.* Philadelphia: Walker and Gillis, 1846.

Gates, Henry Louis Jr., ed. *"Race," Writing, and Difference.* Chicago: University of Chicago Press, 1986.

Giddings, Franklin Henry. *Democracy and Empire.* New York: Macmillan, 1900.

Gilmore, Michael T. *Early American Literature: A Collection of Critical Essays.* Englewood Cliffs, NJ: Prentice-Hall, 1980.

Gleason, Philip. "The Melting Pot: Symbol of Fusion or Confusion?" *American Quarterly* 16 (1964): 20–46.

Gomóra, Francisco López de, in Pietro Martire D'Anghiera. *The Decades of the Newe World or West India.* Translated by Richard Eden. London, 1555. Qtd. in Arber, 338.

Gossett, Thomas F. *Race: The History of an Idea in America*. Dallas: Southern Methodist University Press, 1963.

Gramsci, Antonio. *Selections From the Prison Notebooks*. Edited by and Translated by Quintin Hoare and Geoffrey Nowell Smith. New York: International Publishers, 1972.

Grant, Madison. *The Passing of a Great Race, or the Racial Basis of European History*. New York: Charles Scribner's Sons, 1920.

Grejda, Edward. *The Common Continent of Men: Racial Equality in the Writings of Herman Melville*. Port Washington, NY: Kennikat, 1974.

Gunn, Giles. *Early American Writing*. New York: Penguin, 1994.

Hakluyt, Richard. *The Principal Navigations Voyages Traffiques and Discoveries of the English Nation, Made by Sea or Over-Land to the Remote and Farthest Distant Quarters of the Earth at Any Time Within the Compass of These 1600 Yeeres*. 12 vols. 1903–5. Volume 1. Glasgow: J. MacLehose and Sons, 1903.

Hall, David D. *Worlds of Wonder, Days of Judgment: Popular Religious Belief in Early New England*. New York: Knopf, 1989.

Hall, Kim F. *Things of Darkness: Economies of Race and Gender in Early Modern England*. Ithaca: Cornell University Press, 1995.

Hamilton, Alexander, John Jay, and James Madison. *The Federalist: A Commentary on the Constitution of the United States*. New York: Modern Library, 1982.

Hamilton, Henry. *An Economic Life of Scotland in the 18th Century*. New York: Oxford University Press, 1963.

Hamor, Ralph. *A True Discourse of the Present Estate of Virginia*. London, 1615. Reprint, New York: Da Capo, 1971.

Haney-López, Ian F. *White by Law: The Legal Construction of Race*. New York: New York University Press, 1996.

Hanke, Lewis. *The Spanish Struggle for Justice in the Conquest of America*. Philadelphia: University of Pennsylvania Press, 1949.

Hankins, Frank Hamilton. *The Racial Basis of Civilization: A Critique of the Nordic Doctrine*. New York: Knopf, 1931.

Hening, William Waller, ed. *The Statutes at Large Being a Collection of all the Laws of Virginia from the First Session of the Legislature in the Year 1619*. 18 vols. 1809–1823. Volumes 1–3. Richmond: Samuel Pleasants, 1809.

Hetherington, Hugh W. *Melville's Reviewers: British and American, 1846–1891*. Chapel Hill: University of North Carolina Press, 1961.

Higham, Charles Strachan Sanders. *The Development of the Leeward Islands under the Restoration, 1660–1688: A Study of the Foundations of the Old Colonial System*. Cambridge: Cambridge University Press, 1921.

Hill, Mike, ed. *Whiteness: A Critical Reader*. New York: New York University Press, 1997.

Hillway, Tyrus. "Melville's Use of Two Pseudo-Sciences." *Modern Language Notes*, 64, 3 (1949): 145–50.

Hobsbawm, Eric, and Terence Rauger, eds. *The Invention of Tradition*. Cambridge: Cambridge University Press, 1983.

Holmes, Steven. "Leaving the Suburbs for Rural Areas: Hint of Racial Tension behind a Widespread White Movement." *New York Times*, 19 October 1997, 1:34.

Horsman, Reginald. *Race and Manifest Destiny: The Origins of American Racial Anglo-Saxonism*. Cambridge: Harvard University Press, 1981.

Howe, Daniel Walker. "American Victorianism as a Culture." *American Quarterly* 27 (1975): 507–32.

Hudson, Nicholas. "From 'Nation' to 'Race': The Origin of Racial

Classification in Eighteenth-Century Thought." *Eighteenth-Century Studies* 29, 3 (1996): 247–64.

Huxley, Thomas. "The Methods and Results of Ethnology." *Fortnightly Review* 1 (1865): 267.

James, C. L. R. *Mariners, Renagades and Castaways: The Story of Herman Melville and the World We Live In.* London: Allison and Busby, 1985.

Jameson, Frederick. *The Political Unconscious: Narrative as a Socially Symbolic Act.* Ithaca: Cornell University Press, 1981.

Jefferson, Thomas. *Notes on the State of Virginia.* In *The Portable Thomas Jefferson.* Edited by Merrill D. Peterson. New York: Penguin, 1975.

Jenkins, Edward Sidney. *To Fathom More: African American Scientists and Inventors.* Lanham, MD: University Press of America, 1996.

Johnson, Samuel. *A Journey to the Western Islands of Scotland.* Oxford: Clarendon Press, 1985.

Jordan, Winthrop. *White over Black: American Attitudes toward the Negro, 1550–1812.* Chapel Hill: University of North Carolina Press, 1968.

Karcher, Carolyn. *Shadow over the Promised Land: Slavery, Race, and Violence in Melville's America.* Baton Rouge: Louisiana State University Press, 1980.

Karlsen, Carol F. *The Devil in the Shape of a Woman: Witchcraft in Colonial New England.* New York: Vintage/Random House, 1989.

Koehler, Lyle. *A Search for Power: The "Weaker Sex" in Seventeenth-Century New England.* Chicago: University of Illinois Press, 1980.

Labaree, Leonard W., ed. *The Papers of Benjamin Franklin.* 30 volumes to date. Volume 4. New Haven: Yale University Press, 1961, 225–234.

Lapham, Lewis, "Who and What Is American?" In *The Gray Wolf*

Annual Ten: Changing Community, Edited by Scott Walker. St Paul, MN: Graywolf Press, 1993.

Laquer, Thomas Walter. *Religion and Respectability: Sunday Schools and Working Class Culture, 1780–1850*. New Haven: Yale University Press, 1976.

Levin, Harry. *The Power of Blackness: Hawthorne, Poe, Melville*. New York: Knopf, 1958.

Linnaeus, Carolus. *Caroli Linnaei Systema naturae*. 10th ed. London: British Museum Trustees, 1956.

Maalouf, Amin. *The Crusades through Arab Eyes*. Translated by Jon Rothschild. New York: Schocken Books, 1984.

McIlwaine, Shields. *The Southern Poor-White from Lubberland to Tobacco Road*. New York: Cooper Square Publishers, 1970.

McIntosh, Peggy. "White Privilege and Male Privilege: A Personal Account of Coming to See Correspondences through Work in Women's Studies." In *Race, Class, and Gender: An Anthology*, edited by Margaret L. Andersen and Patricia Hill Collins. Belmont, CA: Wadsworth Publishing Company, 1992.

McWilliams, Carey. *North from Mexico: The Spanish-Speaking People of the United States*. New York: Greenwood, 1990.

Mandel, Bernard. *Labor: Free and Slave, Workingmen and the Antislavery Movement in the United States*. New York: Associated Authors, 1955.

Mather, Cotton. "A Brand Pluck'd Out of the Burning." In Burr, 259–87.

———. *A Good Master Well Served. A Brief Discourse on the Necessary Properties and Practices of a Good Servant*. Boston: B. Green and J. Allen, 1696.

———. *Magnalia Christi Americana*. 1702. Edited by Kenneth B. Murdock. Cambridge: Harvard University Press, 1977.

————. *The Negro Christianized, An Essay to Excite and Assist that Good Work, the Instruction of Negro-Servants in Christianity.* Boston: B. Green, 1706.

————. *Pillars of Salt.* In Williams, *Pillars of Salt*, 64–93.

Maxwell, William H. "School Achievements in New York." *Educational Review* 44 (1912): 288–89.

Melville, Herman. *Moby-Dick, or The Whale.* Edited by Harrison Hayford, Hershel Parker, and G. Thomas Tanselle. Evanston and Chicago: Northwestern University Press and The Newberry Library, 1988.

Miller, Perry. *Errand into the Wilderness.* Cambridge: Harvard University Press, 1953.

————. *Nature's Nation.* Cambridge: Harvard University Press, 1967.

————. *The New England Mind: From Colony to Province.* Cambridge: Harvard University Press, 1953.

Monmonier, Mark. *How to Lie with Maps.* Chicago: University of Chicago Press, 1991.

Morgan, Edmund Sears. *American Slavery, American Freedom: The Ordeal of Colonial Virginia.* New York: Norton, 1975.

————. *The Puritan Family: Religion and Domestic Relations in Seventeenth-Century New England.* New York: Harper, 1966.

Morrison, Toni. *The Bluest Eye.* New York: Plume-Penguin, 1970.

————. *Playing in the Dark: Whiteness and the American Literary Imagination.* New York: Knopf, 1992.

————. "Unspeakable Things Unspoken: The Afro-American Presence in American Literature." *Michigan Quarterly Review* 28, 1 (1989): 1–34.

Morton, Thomas. *New English Canaan of Thomas Morton.* Edited by Charles Francis Adams, Jr. New York: Burt Franklin, 1967.

Myrdal, Gunnar. *An American Dilemma: The Negro Problem and Modern Democracy*. New York: Pantheon, 1962.

Nabokov, Peter, ed. *Native American Testimony: A Chronicle of Indian-White Relations from Prophecy to the Present, 1492–1992*. New York: Penguin, 1991.

Nelson, Dana. *The Word in Black and White: Reading "Race" in American Literature, 1638–1867*. New York: Oxford University Press, 1993.

Nott, Josiah C., and George R. Gliddon. *Types of Mankind: or, Ethnological Researches*. Philadelphia: Lippincott, Grambo, 1854.

Omi, Michael, and Howard Winant. *Racial Formation in the United States: From the 1960s to the 1980s*. New York: Routledge, 1994.

Parsons, Talcott, ed. *Theories of Society: Foundations of Modern Sociological Theory*. 2 vols. Garden City, NY: Free Press of Glencoe, 1961.

Pommer, Henry Francis. *Milton and Melville*. Pittsburgh: University of Pittsburgh Press, 1950.

Pratt, Mara L. *The Later Colonial Period*. Volume 4 of *America's Story for America's Children*. 5 vols. Boston: D. C. Heath, 1901.

Quinn, David B., ed. *America from Concept to Discovery. Early Exploration of North America*. Volume 1 of *New American World: A Documentary History of North America to 1612*. New York: Arno Press and Hector Bye, 1979.

———. *English Plans for North America. The Roanoke Voyages. New England Ventures*. Volume 3 of *New American World: A Documentary History of North America to 1612*. New York: Arno Press and Hector Bye, 1979.

———. *The Extension of Settlement in Florida, Virginia, and Spanish SouthWest*. Volume 5 of *New American World: A Documentary His-*

tory of North America to 1612. New York: Arno Press and Hector Bye, 1979.

Revel, James. "The Poor UNHAPPY Transported FELON'S Sorrowful ACCOUNT of his FOURTEEN [!] Years Transportation, at *Virginia, in America*." *Virginia Magazine of History and Biography* 56 (1948): 187–94.

A Rich Treasure, At an Easy Rate: or, The Ready Way to True Content. Boston: Zechariah Fowle, 1763.

Riis, Jacob. *How the Other Half Lives: Studies among the Tenements of New York*. Boston: St. Martin's, 1996.

———. *The Making of an American*. New York: Grosset and Dunlap, 1901.

Rives, Hallie Erminie. *The Complete Book of Etiquette, with Social Forms for All Ages and Occasions*. Chicago: John C. Winston Company, 1926.

Rodriguez, Richard. *Hunger of Memory: The Education of Richard Rodriguez, an Autobiography*. Boston: David R. Godine, 1982.

Roediger, David, ed. *Towards the Abolition of Whiteness: Essays on Race, Politics, and Working Class History*. London: Verso, 1994.

———. *The Wages of Whiteness: Race and the Making of the American Working Class*. Boston: Routledge, 1991.

Rogin, Michael Paul. *Subversive Genealogy: The Politics and Art of Herman Melville*. New York: Knopf, 1983.

Roosevelt, Theodore. *The Rough Riders*. New York: Charles Scribner's Sons, 1899.

Rowlandson, Mary. *The Captive: The True Story of the Captivity of Mrs. Mary Rowlandson Among the Indians and God's Faithfulness to her in her Time of Trial*. Tucson: American Eagle, 1990.

Rozwenc, Edwin C. "Captain John Smith's Image of America." In Gilmore, 11–21.

Ryan, Joseph, ed. *White Ethnics: Their Life in Working Class America.* Englewood Cliffs, NJ: Prentice-Hall, 1973.

Rydell, Robert. *All the World's a Fair: Visions of Empire at American International Expositions*, 1876–1916. Chicago: University of Chicago Press, 1984.

———. *World of Fairs.* Chicago: University of Chicago Press, 1993.

Rydell, Robert, and Nancy Gwinn, eds. *Fair Representations: World's Fairs and the Modern World.* Amsterdam: VU University Press, 1994.

Said, Edward. *Culture and Imperialism.* New York: Knopf, 1993.

Sarotte, Georges. *Like a Brother, Like a Lover: Male Homosexuality in the American Novel and Theater from Herman Melville to James Baldwin.* Translated by Richard Miller. Garden City, NY: Anchor-Doubleday, 1978.

Saxton, Alexander. *The Rise and Fall of the White Republic: Class Politics and Mass Culture in Nineteenth-Century America.* London: Verso, 1990.

Schlesinger, Arthur M. *Learning How to Behave: A Historical Study of American Etiquette Books.* New York: Cooper Square, 1968.

Scobey, David. "What Shall We Do with Our Walls? The Philadelphia Centennial and the Meaning of Household Design." In Rydell and Gwinn, 87–120.

Shuffleton, Frank, ed. *A Mixed Race: Ethnicity in Early America.* New York: Oxford University Press, 1993.

Siebert, Donald T., Jr. "William Byrd's *Histories of the Line*: The Fashioning of a Hero," *American Literature* 47 (1975): 535–51.

"Slavery in Modern Scotland." *Edinburgh Review* 189 (January 1899): 119–48.

Slotkin, Richard. *Regeneration through Violence: The Mythology of the*

American Frontier, 1600–1860. Middletown, CT: Wesleyan University Press, 1973.

Smith, Henry Nash. *Virgin Land: The American West as Symbol and Myth*. Cambridge: Harvard University Press, 1970.

Smith, John. *A Map of Virginia. With a Description of the Countrey, The Commodities, People, Government and Religion*. Oxford University Press, 1612. Reprint, New York: Da Capo, 1973.

Sollors, Werner. *Beyond Ethnicity: Consent and Descent in American Culture*. New York: Oxford University Press, 1986.

Stoddard, Theodore Lothrop. *The Rising Tide of Color against White World-Supremacy*. New York: Charles Scribner's Sons, 1920.

Stone, Edward. "The Whiteness of the Whale." *College Language Association Journal* 18, 3 (1975): 348–63.

Stowe, Harriet Beecher. *Uncle Tom's Cabin, or, Life among the Lowly*. New York: Penguin, 1981.

Strong, Josiah. *Expansion under New World-Conditions*. New York: Garland, 1971.

Strother, French. "Abraham Cahan, a Leader of the Jews." *World's Work* 26 (1913): 470–74.

Tacitus. *Tacitus' Agricola, Germany and Dialogue on Orators*. Translated by Herbert W. Benario. Norman: University of Oklahoma Press, 1991.

Takaki, Ronald. *Iron Cages: Race and Culture in Nineteenth Century America*. New York: Oxford University Press, 1990.

Thompson, E. P. *The Making of the English Working Class*. New York: Pantheon, 1964.

Thompson, Lawrance Roger. *Melville's Quarrel with God*. Princeton: Princeton University Press, 1952.

Trollope, Frances. *Domestic Manners of the Americans*. New York: Dodd Mead, 1927.

Turner, Sharon. *The History of the Anglo-Saxons, from the Earliest Period to the Norman Conquest.* London: Longman, Brown, Green, and Longman, 1852.

Ulrich, Laurel Thatcher. *Good Wives: Image and Reality in the Lives of Women in Northern New England, 1650–1750.* New York: Knopf, 1982.

Vaughan, Alden T., and Edward W. Clark. *Puritans among the Indians: Accounts of Captivity and Redemption, 1676–1724.* Cambridge: Belknap/Harvard University Press, 1981.

Vick, Marsha, " 'Defamiliarization' and the Ideology of Race in *Moby Dick.*" *College Language Association Journal* 35, 3 (1992): 325–38.

Virginia County Record. *Northumberland County Record Book, 1652–58* (21 July 1656); *Northumberland County Order Book* (20 January 1655).

Vitruvius. *The Ten Books on Architecture.* Translated by Morris Hickey Morgan. New York: Dover, 1960.

Wald, Lillian D. *The House on Henry Street.* New York: Dover, 1971.

Wells, Robert W. *The Population of the British Colonies in America before 1776: A Survey of the Census Data.* Princeton: Princeton University Press, 1975.

Welter, Barbara. *Dimity Convictions: The American Woman in the Nineteenth Century.* Athens: Ohio University Press, 1976.

Whitmore, William H., and William S. Appleton, eds. *Hutchinson Papers.* 2 vols. Volume 1. New York: Burt Franklin, 1967.

Wilkins, Thurman. *Cherokee Tragedy: The Ridge Family and the Decimation of a People.* Norman: University of Oklahoma Press, 1986.

Williams, Daniel E. "The Gratification of That Corrupt and Lawless Passion: Character Types and Themes in Early New England Rape Narratives." In Shuffleton, 194–221.

————. *Pillars of Salt: An Anthology of Early American Criminal Narratives*. Madison, WI: Madison House, 1993.

Winthrop, John. *Winthrop's Journal, "History of New England," 1630–1649*. Edited by James Kendall Hosmer. 2 vols. Volume 1. New York: Charles Scribner's Sons, 1908.

Wister, Owen. *The Virginian: A Horseman of the Plains*. New York: Macmillan, 1902.

Wood, Gordon S. *The Creation of the American Republic, 1776–1787*. New York: Norton, 1972.

Wright, Nathalia. *Melville's Use of the Bible*. New York: Octagon Books, 1969.

Wrobel, Arthur, ed. *Pseudo-Science and Society in Nineteenth-Century America*. Lexington: University Press of Kentucky, 1987.

Wrobel, Paul. "Becoming a Polish American: A Personal Point of View." In Ryan, 52–58.

Index

About the Author

Valerie Babb is currently Professor of English at Georgetown University where she teaches courses in American literature, Women's Studies, and American Studies. She has also been a faculty member of the Bread Loaf School of English, Middlebury College. She has written extensively in the fields of African American literature and culture and is author of *Ernest Gaines* (1991); co-author of *Black Georgetown Remembered* (1992), a history of African American community of Georgetown, Washington, DC.; and co-producer of the documentary video, *Black Georgetown Remembered* (1989).